What others have said...

A perfect recipe to elevate your career.
"If you want to learn how to boost your career, this book is for you. This book presents well-established concepts to differentiate yourself from the crowded workforce market. It is equipped with all needed information that is required not only for a better career but also for a successful one."
—**Imran Khan**
Senior IT Consultant, Sondhi Solutions

A must-read primer.
"Jeffrey S. Ton has written a must-read primer for anyone engaged in a job transition or contemplating a new job search…Read this book—and learn from one of the best."
—**Ken Bryan**
Fractional CxO, Husker Consulting

Networking works!
"Working in the information technology industry for over thirty years, I have found different points in my life where it was necessary to seek new employment, whether this transition meant promotion, travel, work/life balance, or being let go by a previous employer. The one constant in finding new opportunities was my method of finding it. Many consider the typical avenues: job search engines, headhunters/recruiters, personal contacts, business social forums, and formal networks. Personally, every opportunity I have found has been through networking. There are personal contacts, networking forums such as LinkedIn, or the source of my latest position, the Indy CIO Network. To put this in perspective, I accepted a position several years ago entailing frequent travel, which diverted my attention away from local networking. When the time came to eye local employment, it consumed roughly three months. After working locally for a

few years, using the networking techniques found in *Amplify Your Job Search*, I rebuilt my local network, enabling me to locate a perfect match in only three weeks."

—Rob Brinkman
Director of Data Architecture, CNO Financial Group

Top ten lists landed my dream job!

"Jeff advised me to create a list of criteria using the *Amplify Your Job Search* Top Ten Lists described in his book and use them to compare potential employers during my recent job search. This exercise helped me better understand what a dream job was for me and gave me confidence to wait for the right fit. I'm happy to say it worked, and I start an amazing new position next week!"

—Brad Long
Information Systems Manager, Young & Laramore

Crank up your volume.

"Jeff's new book *Amplify Your Job Search: Strategies for Finding Your Dream Job* speaks to cranking up the volume of your job search. You will put new tools in your tool belt to help you by defining your dream job, building a strong professional network, and identifying employers who have your dream job waiting! Jeff has spoken to Passport to Employment in Indianapolis (a job seekers' networking group) on numerous occasions and is always well received leaving nuggets behind that make a difference."

—Patti Quiring
Retired, Quiring Associates (a custom search and recruitment firm)

Tackle the hurdles and roadblocks.

"In *Amplify Your Job Search: Strategies for Finding Your Dream Job*, author Jeff Ton takes the reader on a journey and reveals a framework to find, not just a job, but the job. Using a series of tools he calls Amplifiers, Ton guides the reader each step of the way. Finding a job is hard work. However, Jeff's casual and conversational tone helps the reader face the hurdles and roadblocks. This is a must-read for anyone seeking their dream job!"

—**Amy Waninger**
Author of *Network beyond Bias*

The urgency of professional networking.

"In his book *Amplify Your Job Search*, Jeff highlights the urgency of professional networking not only to your job search but to your career. As he points out, while you are in transition, joining a job seekers group can provide guidance and support to you while you conduct your search. Jeff has presented these concepts to TNG, a job seekers networking group and helped their members find their dream jobs. With this book, many others will find strategies to guide them in their search."

—**Dale Hinshaw**
CEO OmniHR Consulting

Passion for people.

"Jeff's passion for people shines as he presents his experience and wisdom in an approachable and friendly manner. Even if you are not looking to change jobs, his insights are valuable, and his practical guidance can genuinely help you amplify who you are."

—**Ben Miller**
Senior Cloud Solutions Architect and Author of *Like Minds*

Sound, practical advice.

"Based on real-life experiences together with sound, practical advice, Jeff's book is a great guide to finding your next job. And not just any job, but your dream job. So often, job seekers don't take the time to reflect, self-assess, and really dive into what they want and need in a job. Jeff walks the reader through all the steps they need to take to manage their career successfully. He discusses the emotional rollercoaster of job searching and provides a structure to help make the whole process more manageable. Whether you're looking for another job by choice or necessity, *Amplify Your Job Search* will be a useful guide for you."

—Cathy Ginsberg
President, Coach, and Trainer, People Focus Training

The good of talent acquisition.

"In *Amplify Your Job Search*, Jeff shares his knowledge and expertise. The book provides a very thorough path for the reader to follow. My 20+ years of experience are from both sides of the career negotiating table. I know the good, the bad, and the ugly of talent acquisition. I speak as a candidate, advisory recruiter, career exploration, and job search strategy coach. Readers should not have any concerns finding their dream job after reading this book."

—KayLee Haw
Career Exploration Coach

Jeff Ton has successfully done it again!

"*Amplify Your Job Search* by Jeff Ton, who also authored the book *Amplify Your Value*, has successfully done it again! It is such an easy read, and it walks you through a journey of how to find your next opportunity. While your next position might not be your dream job, the techniques Ton offers, along with specific guidelines and strategies, may get you really close! You will understand how to effectively use your social network, establish warm introductions from your network, and how to effectively journal as a means to becoming that much more successful in landing your next opportunity and so much more! Ton can relate to those who have lost their job, those who were a part of a reduction in force, those who search for other opportunities while working… the list goes on. He will teach you that you are not alone and show you how he can relate to the different situations you may be in. You will be able to go all the way back to when you graduated high school and remember what your summer job was, if you had a summer job. You will be able to journey back to all of the organizations with which you were affiliated, including the military and college. The learning opportunity here is to recall all of the above and include the details in your Accomplishment Amplifier. What is an Accomplishment Amplifier? You will find that out and more while reading *Amplify Your Job Search*. If you are looking to level up your career, if you are in the middle of a job search, or if you are currently working and need another challenge, I highly recommend *Amplify Your Job Search* in order to land that next best opportunity."

Stephanie Gilbert
Talent Acquisition Manager, Givelify

Understand where you have been.

"There are two ways to go about the search for your next job: taking a shotgun approach and taking the time to evaluate where you have been and what you have accomplished, then building a detailed plan that will be laser-focused on making a move. Ton applies best practices developed over a decades-long career of success. Told in a conversational style designed to help you get to your best role, following his advice will not only help you land your next job, it will set you up on a track to build your career over the long-haul. And the chapter on networking makes the book worth buying on its own!"

—Kenn Beckwith
Managing Director, Experis Account Management at Experis/Manpower Group

Excellent strategy and step-by-step approach.
"In *Amplify Your Job Search*, Jeff has laid out an excellent strategy and step-by-step approach on how to self-identify what you really want in your next position and how to showcase the real value you will bring to your next company by creating pointed profiles, resumes, and brand to express it correctly. However, the real power of this book is in the step-by-step plan of marketing yourself and proactively targeting the market and the specific companies that have the types of opportunities you are interested in. If you are seeking a new opportunity, this is a must read on how to understand exactly what you want, how to express what you really offer, along with how to develop a strong, proactive plan to successfully identify and land your next dream job."

—**Eric J. Miller**
Managing Director, Centerline Solutions, Inc.

AMPLIFY YOUR JOB SEARCH

Also by Jeffrey S. Ton

BOOKS
Amplify Your Value
https://jeffreyston.com/author-amplify-your-value

BLOGS
Rivers of Thought
https://riversofthought.net

People Development Magazine
https://peopledevelopmentmagazine.com/author/jeff-ton

Intel IT Peer Network
https://itpeernetwork.intel.com/author/jtongici

Institute for Digital Transformation
https://www.institutefordigitaltransformation.org/digital-era-now

Forbes Technology Council
https://www.forbes.com/sites/forbestechcouncil/people/jeffreyton

AMPLIFY YOUR JOB SEARCH

Strategies for
Finding Your Dream Job

JEFFREY S. TON

Published by Ton Enterprises, LLC

Copyright 2020 © Ton Enterprises, LLC
All rights reserved. No part of this book may be reproduced or transmitted in any form or by any means, electronic or mechanical, including photocopying, recording or by any information storage and retrieval system without written permission of the publisher, except for the inclusion of brief quotations in a review.

Cover Design: Jennifer Vogel
Interior Design: Lori Paximadis
Graphic Design: Jennifer Vogel
Amplify Dial Image: Copyright Le Moal Olivier

Ton Enterprises LLC
7575 Sargent Road
Indianapolis, IN 46256

Trade Paper ISBN: 978-1-7353090-0-2
Digital ISBN: 978-1-7353090-1-9
Library of Congress Control Number: 2020913199

To L. Eugene Ton.
My dad. My teacher.
My guide. My pastor.

My best friend.

I miss you.

Contents

Foreword by Phil Rosenberg — xv
Acknowledgments — xix
Introduction — xxiii

1. It Starts with You — 1
2. What's Your Sign? — 11
3. You've Accomplished a Lot! — 29
4. It Begins and Ends with Your Network — 45
5. The Ins and Outs of Networking — 61
6. Your Resume (It's About Time!) — 73
7. Marketing—with a Twist — 103
8. Ready? Set? Go! — 113
9. Let's Get Creative — 127
10. The First Date and Beyond — 135
11. The End Game — 145

Bibliography — 151
Resources — 153
About the Author — 157

Foreword

Finding a job can be hard work in the best of times. In this time of high unemployment, it can seem like a monumental task. I've been one of the industry's most sought-after national recruiters for over sixteen years. I've also been a career coach helping tens of thousands of professionals beat unemployment for over thirteen years. As an internationally published career advice author, I've seen both sides of the employment desk. This perspective enables me to help my clients succeed where others fail.

I launched reCareered in one of the worst job markets in our lifetimes. I coached numerous people. I heard the heartbreaking stories. Around the time Jeff discovered my blog and newsletter, I was talking to people on a weekly basis who were about to lose their homes. And this time will be worse. During a recession, my goal is to help people improve their career and avoid losing their homes. I want to help them to transition into a job that's as least as good as the one they were in—and potentially a job that's better than the one they left. It requires a different process. It requires a different type of resume. Most importantly, it requires a plan.

I was thrilled to learn that my advice through my website reCareered was foundational to Jeff Ton's career search over ten years ago. After hearing his story of finding my work and leveraging it to find his dream job, I couldn't wait to read his book, *Amplify Your Job Search: Strategies for Finding Your Dream Job*. It did not disappoint. I have read a lot of really bad job search books. There's a lot of very basic to kindergarten-level advice that confuses and frustrates people. They give people bad direction, which causes them to work on a job search based on random applications, volume, and luck. That's not even a great strategy during good job markets. In a recession, it's a strategy for losing your house.

That's not this book. This book is one of the one of the best books I've ever read in this space. This book is a great resource for the job seeker, especially for the specific audience of networking fearing professionals.

If you've read *What Color Is Your Parachute*, you are going to love *Amplify Your Job Search*. In my opinion, that book fell a bit short. It was a bit esoteric and created a lot of nice ideas and thoughts in people's minds. But it didn't give an action plan. It leaves the reader wondering, *How do I actually do that? Amplify Your Job Search* gives the reader an actionable plan.

From the outset, this book provides readers with the tools and the process they need to succeed in their job search, from journaling and networking to using the data-driven approach of the Amplifiers. Not having a plan for your job search is a recipe for personal economic disaster. This book provides you with that plan.

This book will encourage you to dig deep. You will learn a lot about yourself through the Personal Brand Amplifier. Using the Accomplishment Amplifier and the Resume Amplifier, you will discover aspects of your career that could unlock your dream job. As someone with over 37,000 connections on LinkedIn, I believe in the power of a professional network. You will find that the Network Amplifier and Jeff's advice on networking will outlive your job search; it has the power to be a career changer. As he explains in his laser approach, knowing your target market can be the difference between finding a job and finding *the* job.

Jeff's casual, conversational style makes this book an easy read. He is able to convey complex concepts in a very understandable and relatable manner. His background as a technology executive shines through in this book. His ability to define a plan and guide the reader through the execution of the plan comes from his years of experience guiding technology departments and companies. However, this is a not just a book for IT professionals. This book is for any professional looking to improve their career trajectory. His experience as both a hiring manager and a job seeker provides valuable insights along the way.

The journey ahead will be difficult, but with Jeff as your guide, I have no doubt you will succeed.

—Phil Rosenberg
President, reCareered
LinkedIn's most connected career coach,
recruiter, and author

Acknowledgments

The book you are about to read is a culmination of more than two decades of being a hiring manager, a job seeker, and a mentor to those in transition. As a hiring manager, I have read countless resumes, interviewed hundreds of candidates, and hired dozens of professionals. In my own searches, I have been on the other side of the desk, so to speak. Writing, rewriting, and rewriting again my resume. Preparing for and participating in countless interviews. And negotiating and landing a half-dozen jobs. I have mentored dozens of professionals while they navigated their transitions. I only hope they learned as much from me as I did from them.

Over the last ten years, I have recommended the strategies you will find between these covers. I would be remiss if I did not call out three resources that proved to be invaluable to me in my searches and that I have recommended to others in the years since.

The first is *The Executive Job Search: A Comprehensive Handbook for Seasoned Professionals* by Orrin G. Wood. Wood's book provided the foundation for my search ten years ago. You will find reference to his work in the section titled "PAR: It's Not Just for Golf" in chapter 3.

Second is the book *How to Find a Job on LinkedIn, Facebook, Twitter, and Google+* by Brad and Debra Schepp. I must confess, when I read the book it referenced MySpace instead of Google+. I was facing a job search for the first time. Not only had I never really needed to look for a job before (the next one was always right there), but I had certainly never used social media to aid in my search. The Schepps' work helped me to leverage those platforms to land my dream job.

The other resource I used and continue to recommend is the website reCareered. Phil Rosenberg is LinkedIn's most connected career coach and recruiter. On reCareered Phil has built the web's central hub for job search advice. I found the advice and insight to be instrumental to my search. Phil now does free webinars where he shares his knowledge weekly. His website has an archive that is a goldmine to any job seeker.

The people who have helped me in my own search and career are numerous. I want to call out a few with a special thank-you: John Frank, whose advice to use a laser approach led me to my dream job. Patti Quiring, who helped me tune my LinkedIn profile and taught me some tricks to using LinkedIn. Josh Hill, who not only taught me the phrase "hard hat and muddy boots" as a way to lead, but also sent me the job description of my dream job. Elaine Bedel, whom I hadn't talked to in twenty years, yet dropped everything to meet for coffee, share her insights, and provide a reference for my dream job. Wayne Patrick, who not only went out of his way to meet me for coffee and provide a reference, but has become a mentor and a friend. Jim Andreoni, who was the chief information officer for the largest organization in Goodwill Industries International's membership yet,

ACKNOWLEDGMENTS

took time to talk to me, share insights, and provide a path to lead an organization for me to follow. Eric Miller, one of the busiest tech recruiters in Indianapolis, who has helped me and countless others find the path to our future jobs, many times pro bono. Bill Lay, for writing one of the greatest lines on a resume I have ever seen! (Hey, you have to read the book to learn the line.)

I want to acknowledge two people who have been key to my knowledge of recruiting, interviewing, hiring, offer evaluation, and all things HR. The first is Katie Gaffin. Katie is chief executive officer at Alpha Chi Omega Fraternity. She is one of the hardest working and most wickedly smart people I have ever known. She has mentored, taught, and retaught me about HR and leadership for two decades.

The second is Carmen Ton, my wife. Her impact on my life would take volumes to describe. Her knowledge of recruiting, team building, account management, benefits, and countless other topics helped me to build my first team and propelled my career into executive management. This book—heck, this career—would not have been possible without her by my side, first as a business associate, then as a friend, and ultimately as my wife.

Thank you to all of you. Thank you to the countless others I did not name. Your impact on my life and on my career has meant the world to me!

Introduction

If you are reading this, chances are you are "in transition," "in between jobs," or "undergoing a career change." You may find yourself in this position for the first time in your career, or perhaps you've been in this situation before. In any case, you are without a job and are looking for advice on how and where to find your next one.

I've talked with dozens, if not hundreds, of people just like you who are between jobs and searching for the next one. It can be lonely. It can be scary. It can be depressing. I spoke with someone recently whose search has been in progress for six months. She is the major breadwinner in her household. She was scared, and yes, she was depressed.

You may currently have a job and are seeking a new one, perhaps one that is more fulfilling, pays more, or provides an opportunity to move up the career ladder. You might have been with your current company for five to ten years or more, perhaps you've been there less than five years and feel it's time for a change, or you might have joined your company less than a year ago and have realized it is not right for you. Like your colleague who is between jobs, you would like some tips and tricks to land that new role.

I recently talked with an information technology leader who had been in the same job for twelve years. He ran IT for a mid-sized manufacturing company. As he talked about his recent decision to start searching for something new, I asked him about his current role. "It's okay, I guess. I'm just looking for new challenges, new opportunities. I've been in manufacturing for twelve years, and I don't even like manufacturing." No wonder he was interested in changing jobs!

You may be in a dead-end job, one that sucks the life out of you. You wake up on Monday morning exhausted and dreading going to work. Every day is like the movie *Groundhog Day*, just another day of the same sh—er, uh, stuff. I have news for you: It doesn't have to be that way. You can find a job that gets you excited, one where you cannot wait to get to the office, one that ignites your passion. It's true! It takes work, but given you spend at least a third of your day doing your job, wouldn't it be great to enjoy it?

I had a conversation with someone who was a year removed from such a job. He had a role the required him to be available 24/7. It was a high-pressure, low-paying position. He hated work. His stomach was in knots from the anxiety of his position. He quit with no new job lined up. He put his health and marriage over financial stability. Using the strategies found in this book, he now has his dream job. He is a completely different person.

How do you approach your search? What strategies do you employ?

Shotgun or Laser: The Choice Is Yours

When I was in transition several years ago, one of my mentors, John Frank, chief operating officer of United-

HealthOne, a division of UnitedHealth Group, told me, "There are really only two ways to find a job: a shotgun approach or a laser approach." He went on to explain that a shotgun approach to a job search is one in which you are searching for a job, just about any job. Yes, you may have some parameters, such as it must be white collar, it must be within your skill set, or perhaps even in your locality. But you are not looking for a specific role within a specific industry. You may be applying for positions that range from individual contributor roles to executive management roles.

With a laser approach, you are zeroed in on a specific role, in specific industries, and perhaps even at specific organizations. You know exactly the type of job you want. You have a process to find that job, and you may pass up opportunities that don't align with your focus.

Both searches are effective and will land you a position. The laser approach may take longer to bear fruit; however, I believe (and John believed) that by taking the laser approach, the role you end up with will be far more rewarding and fulfilling, your boss and you will be more likely to see eye-to-eye, and you will feel more a part of the company than one found by a shotgun approach. In fact, using the laser approach can help you land your dream job!

It will come as no surprise that this book focuses on the laser approach. In it, you will find a guide to finding your next position. While no one can guarantee success in finding and landing a job, much less your dream job, the steps and techniques described in this book have worked. I have used these strategies to land my dream job, and dozens of others have as well. These strategies are a culmination of insights from professionals around the country through their books, blog posts, and podcasts; countless conversations with mentors and coaches, thought leaders, and executives (like John); and dozens, if not hundreds, of coffee meetings with professionals in transition over the last ten years.

There is no silver bullet. You will not find a magic answer within these pages. Finding work is…well, work. Your job for the next several weeks and possibly months is to find a job. But not just *a* job—*the* job. The job that will make you feel rewarded and valued, aligns with your values and goals, and will take your career to the places you have always aspired to go.

Network Your Way

As you may have heard, job searching begins and ends with your network. Over 80 percent of jobs are filled through professional networking. The old adage "It's not what you know but who you know" is true in a sense. While that saying might have a bad rap in years past and ring of nepotism and cronyism, that is not the case these days (I'm not naive enough to think that doesn't happen, but I do believe that to be rare). A warm introduction from someone in your network can separate you from the stack of resumes in someone's inbox and get you a longer look, perhaps even that first interview. After that, it's up to you!

What makes this book different from others you might have read is that it's not written by an outplacement counselor, recruiter, or headhunter. It's written by someone who has been there and done that. Someone who has experienced job-hunting bumps and bruises. Someone who has experienced the depression, desperation, and feelings of low self-worth that some people will experience in their job search.

My Transition Story

In 2009, after almost thirty years in the workforce, twelve of those years with one company and fourteen years with another, I was working at a commercial real estate development firm. It was going to be my last job. I was chief information officer, the top role for a career information technology professional. We were growing like gangbusters when I joined the firm in 2006 and would more than double in size over the next two years. I had no need for a professional network; I was going to retire from that place—early, maybe even at fifty. Besides, I didn't have time to meet people for coffee, lunch, or drinks, because I was putting in twelve-hour days, five or six days a week.

And then 2008 hit, and everything changed. The financial crisis. The bank meltdown. Commercial real estate fell off a cliff. By the time 2009 dawned, what was once a firm of 450 employees had fewer than 200 and was spiraling toward 50. My department of 25 was now a department of 3. I was able to negotiate a contract to go part-time during 2009 and lead the negotiation for downsizing of our technology contracts. By fall, I was unemployed. After trying to start my own business (2009 was not the best time to start a business), I realized I needed a job.

I had not had to look for a job in more than twenty years. The next one was always right there. In the age of the internet and social media, I had no idea where to even start. I started making phone calls, engaged an executive coach, read some books, and connected with mentors (like John).

During my search I was amazed at the response to my requests for help. Friends and family, of course, stepped in to help and talk. Professional colleagues asked how they could help. People I had not spoken to in more than twenty years said yes, they could meet. People I had never met said yes, let's do coffee and talk. In the months of my job search not. one. person. said. no!

When I landed my job, I made myself two promises. Promise number one: I will never ever let my network grow cold again. You never know when you will need it. Today, my professional network connections number in the thousands. Promise number two: Whenever anyone asks, my answer is "Let's do coffee. When and where do you want to meet?" During the COVID-19 outbreak, these "coffees" turned to virtual coffees over Zoom. I continue to have a lot of virtual coffees even as businesses open back up.

Amplify Your Job Search **Framework**

Amplify Your Job Search details the framework and the process I used to successfully find my dream job. It is the same process I have shared with countless professionals like you over the last ten years. Those who implemented this process successfully found jobs—some in a matter of weeks, some after a few months.

Finding your dream job begins by looking inside. In chapter 1, "It Starts with You," I'm going to introduce you to your first tool: your Transition Journal. I am going ask you to journal…a lot! If you are new to journaling, I provide step-by-step instructions. Throughout this book you will find journal prompts to guide your reflection on the process.

In chapter 2, "What's Your Sign?," we will use the first

of several "Amplifiers," the Personal Brand Amplifier™, to help you define your personal brand. You will gain an understanding of your strengths, values, passions, and purpose.

In chapter 3, "You've Accomplished a Lot!," we will use the Accomplishment Amplifier™ to capture all that you have accomplished over your career to this moment in time. This will serve as the foundation for your resume. Even if you have an existing resume, you will want to complete this exercise.

The Network Amplifier™ is introduced in chapter 4, "It Begins and Ends with Your Network." I'll discuss the different types of networks and the role they play in your search for your dream job. Spoiler alert: They are important—almost vital.

All of us can use some tips and tricks to effective networking. In chapter 5, "The Ins and Outs of Networking," I provide some best practices. Even the most avid networker will pick up a few nuggets.

Your resume serves a key purpose in your search. In chapter 6, "Your Resume (It's about Time!)," we uncover that purpose. Your Resume Amplifier™ will serve as the foundation for your resume. You will revisit this tool often. This tool will also help you to build the four (yes, four) different kinds of resumes you will need.

As chapter 7, "Marketing—with a Twist," explains, you are now in sales and marketing. You are selling…you. We will explore some of the fundamentals of marketing as we determine your target market. Hint: Those are the companies that have your dream job waiting! The SOM Amplifier™ and its cousin the SAM List™ will guide the rest of our journey together.

Chapter 8, "Ready? Set? Go!," will bring it all together

as you begin the process of networking, applying, and interviewing for your dream job. You will learn the value of your social media networks and the important role they play in this leg of your journey.

Aptly titled chapter 9, "Let's Get Creative," provides some creative ideas to further help you and your resume stand out from the crowd. Use these suggestions as is or use them as a springboard to come up with your own creative ideas.

As you begin dating—I mean, interviewing, chapter 10, "The First Date and Beyond," will help you prepare for the interview. You may, in fact, be the most prepared candidate your new company will see.

We end our journey together with a few words about evaluating and negotiating an offer, or multiple offers. Chapter 11, "The End Game," will guide you through using the SOM Amplifier to compare offers and determine if an offer is, in fact, the offer for your dream job. I will also offer some guidance on what to do after you have landed your dream job.

Your Journey

You are embarking on a journey. It will be challenging. It will be frustrating. However, when successful, it will also be rewarding. You will be stronger and better equipped to handle the challenges ahead. I'm going to ask you to dig deep. For some, this will be way outside your comfort zone. I encourage you to get comfortable with being uncomfortable.

We are going to spend a lot of time in reflection, especially in the first part of the book. If this isn't your thing, I urge you to power through nonetheless. Like the rhythm section of a great rock band, this reflection is going to serve as the backbone as we build the harmonies and the melody for you to rock your way to your dream job.

Are you ready? I hope so, because your journey starts… with you!

1

It Starts with You

You've been terminated. Laid off. RIFed. Fired. Time to blow the digital dust off your resume, add this most recent position to it, and start mailing it out! Right?

Wrong! Whether you are in transition between jobs, or you are currently employed and have made the decision to start a search, our work starts with you. How are you? No, really. Don't say fine. You are not. Whether it has been forced on you by circumstances or you've come to this decision yourself, you are embarking on one of the most challenging aspects of your career: a job search. Are you angry? Are you bitter? Are you disillusioned? Scared? Nervous? Anxious? Uncertain?

It's okay! We humans are emotional beings. It is okay to own your emotions. In these early stages of your search, we are going to focus a lot on you, what you are feeling, and what you are thinking. Spend some time now to explore those feelings and thoughts.

Perhaps you've been laid off due to a reduction in force (RIF) brought about by the COVID-19 pandemic or for some other less dramatic reason. You didn't deserve it! You were a solid performer! Why wasn't Joe or Sally let go?

Or perhaps you were called into your boss's office one day, out of the blue, and she told you, "We're going in a different direction," or "Your performance is not meeting expectations," or "You are not driving the results we need." Seriously? You? You were doing your job. Don't they know the work you did every day? Why didn't someone tell you that you needed to step up your game?

Maybe you made a mistake and went afoul of a policy. You grabbed a six-pack of soft drinks from the company-stocked fridge and took it home; everybody does it. What? You've been fired? No warning? No second chance? Why are they singling you out as the example to make?

You've been at this company for several years. You feel it's time for a change. You're not sure why, but you are bored with your current assignments. You've spoken to your boss, but either they don't listen, or they have no other work for you. Surely, over at Acme the work is far more exciting. Maybe the grass is greener.

You may feel your work is worth a higher salary. The 3.5 percent raise you've gotten each of the last five years isn't cutting it. Heck, with inflation, you've lost money. You know the market value of your position is much higher. Last week over dinner, Bill mentioned his salary. It confirmed your suspicion: He is making far more than you, and you are in similar lines of work.

Perhaps your boss has unreasonable expectations. You have been busting your hump to try to get it all done. She keeps adding more to your plate. Your team is near revolt. They are stressed. You are stressed. You've raised your concerns. She just won't listen…and adds more. You must make a change before you explode.

No matter your reasons, you need to examine them. No matter the situation, there are always lessons to learn, lessons about yourself, your career, and your motivations.

Transition Journal

One of the best ways to examine your situation and learn the lessons is to journal. As you proceed through the steps in this book, I'd like you to journal. It's not as hard as it sounds. I will guide you along the way. You do not need to be a writer to write a journal. No one is going to read it. It is for your eyes only.

Even if you are already an avid journaler, you are still going to want to read this section. There will be some specific things you will want to know about your Transition Journal.

There are many benefits to writing in a journal. In his post "10 Surprising Benefits You'll Get from Keeping a Journal" on Huffington Post, contributor Thai Nguyen describes some of the benefits you will get from journaling. At least three (and probably all ten) will help you in your transition: achieving goals (your goal is to find a new job), healing (you may not be physically injured or ill, but you have probably suffered a trauma), and self-confidence (you may be questioning yourself and your skills right now).

I'd like to add a couple more benefits to the list. Keeping a journal can help you process what has just happened. You want to work through those emotions before you start to network for your next position and certainly before you go on your first interview. You need to make sense of what has just happened. Writing it down gives you the ability to reflect on your thoughts, feelings, and plans. You can refer to your writing to see how your thoughts, feelings, and plans have evolved over time.

The other benefit I'd like to point out is that a journal helps keep you organized. You will be busy in the days and weeks to come. It will be easy to forget some things and misremember others. Having a record of your daily thoughts and activities will help you to keep it all straight.

There are many different types of journaling. In fact, an internet search for "types of journals" returns dozens of articles about types of journals, including "17 Types of Journals to Keep Your Life Organized," "5 Different Types of Journaling and How to Select Best One for You," and "7 Different Types of Journals with Examples." In its simplest form, a journal is a written record of something. It might be a food journal, a weight loss journal, a bullet journal, or a dream journal. For our purposes, your Transition Journal will be a place to keep track of your transition journey: your thoughts, feelings, insights, and ideas along the way.

Just as there are many types of journals, there are different ways to journal. You can put pen to paper and write a physical journal, or you can put fingers to keys and keep a digital journal. You might choose to use a journal app, a leather-bound journal, a pad of paper, or the swag journal from the last conference you attended. I am going to encourage you to handwrite your journal. There are many benefits to writing in a physical journal. It forces you to slow down and be mindful. Studies have shown the act of writing forces your brain to focus on what is important (see the article by Virginia W. Berninger et al. in the bibliography for the results of one such study). With all that said, the *act* of journaling is more important than the *how* for our purposes. I'd rather you journal in whatever form (written, digital, video) you need to journal to form the habit and be consistent than not journal at all.

The Habit of Journaling

If you are new to journaling, developing the habit is easy. As you begin the process, there are five key elements to keep in mind.

The **frequency** with which you journal is important. To help form the habit, set a specific cadence. For our purposes, your cadence should be at least once a day. While frequency is important, don't beat yourself up if you miss a day here and there throughout the journey.

When you journal will be a matter of personal preference. Regardless of when, set a specific time of day and stick with it. Knowing you have a designated time will help to form the habit. You will need ten to thirty minutes each day (including Saturday and Sunday). For me, personally, I find early mornings are best. The house is quiet, and the whirlwind of the day has not yet encompassed me. If you are a morning person, try setting your alarm (you are still setting an alarm, right?) ten minutes earlier every few days until you are getting up thirty minutes earlier than normal, and then spend those minutes writing in your journal. For you night owls, carve out some quiet time late in the day for reflecting in your journal.

Place can be a great tool to center our thoughts and set the mood for journaling. Journaling in the same place each day also helps to create the habit. I use my home office; others may want to sit in their favorite comfy chair or on the couch.

Knowing what to write in your journal can, at times, be the most difficult. Theodore Roosevelt kept extensive journals throughout his life. Once, on a very tragic day, he merely wrote a large X on the page. No further explanation was needed. Your Transition Journal is more than just a daily diary of your activities of the day, though that is a good place to start. The journal is yours. Through the remainder of this book, I will help guide your writing with some prompting questions.

Reflect on Your Journal

The primary purpose of a journal is to keep a record of your thoughts and activities. However, once written, it should not just sit on a shelf. Reread portions of your journal periodically. What stands out for you? Do you feel the same about a given event a week later, or a month later? What did you learn from the event in retrospect?

Getting Started with the Transition Journal

To start your journal, write your story. Don't worry about the quality of your prose or your storytelling abilities; just write. Use as many pages as you'd like. Where were you born? What was your family like? Where did you go to school? Who were your friends? What was your first job? What did you like about it? What didn't you like? Why did you leave that job for the next one? Repeat those last four questions for each position you have held throughout your career, until you get to the most recent.

Tell the story of your most recent position. Why did you leave? Or, if you are still there, why are you considering a change? Use one or two of the circumstances described earlier in this chapter to serve as your guide. Be brutally honest, with yourself and about the company. Be as blunt as you want—it's your journal. Think back over the past weeks or months. Were there signs?

It may sound silly to start at the beginning of your story. You may think you don't have a story to tell. But trust me, you do, even if you are just telling yourself. There will be themes in your story. There will be facts you uncover you can use later. It will help you to process. You will thank me later.

Bookmark this page. Go spend time with your journal. This first set of entries will be important. The rest of this chapter can wait.

Strengths and Weaknesses

The advice to maximize your strengths and make your weaknesses irrelevant is often attributed to Peter Drucker. This advice has been used to train managers, executives, and leaders to focus on their strengths, ignoring their weaknesses in the hopes of making their weaknesses irrelevant. We have done a disservice to several generations of leaders. How, you ask? By not also sharing this quote from Drucker: "Cultivate a deep understanding of yourself—not only what your strengths and weaknesses are but also how you learn, how you work with others, what your values are, and where you can make the greatest contribution. Because only when you operate from strengths can you achieve true excellence."

We've all taken countless assessments: StrengthsFinder, DiSC, Myers-Briggs, Enneagram, PAIRIN, Kolbe, and more. You may have taken some of these more than once. They are all incredibly valuable. However, if you are like me, you don't have a copy of the results from any of them. (I am going to share a fantastic offer later in this chapter that will fix that problem going forward!) I am going to suggest that you take one or two assessments, but as you will see, I am also going to recommend that you work with a career coach or an executive coach, and they will probably have a preference for which ones they would like you to take.

It is important that you have a deep understanding of

your strengths and weaknesses—in fact, it's more than important; it's imperative. Too many times we tend to assume we know what our strengths and weaknesses are. But if we don't take the time to have a deep understanding, we may miss strengths, miss weaknesses, or miscategorize one as the other. While any of those errors could have consequences, the miscategorization of a strength or a weakness could impact the trajectory of your career.

In the book *Leadership and Self-Deception*, the Arbinger Institute describes a little-known problem that can be the root of many organizational problems (and some personal ones, too): self-deception, a systemic distortion of oneself and others. Through the fictional story of Tom and his career at Zagrum, the authors describe self-deception and the problems it causes. Lucky for us, they also describe how to overcome it.

For our purposes we are going to focus on self-examination. You must look at yourself without any of the guises of self-deception, hold yourself up to scrutiny, and truly understand your strengths and your weaknesses. If you don't do this, you may be trying to maximize a strength that isn't your greatest strength, or you could ignore your weaknesses in an attempt to make them irrelevant, when that trait may be the key to your success.

Take out your Transition Journal. Write a list of your strengths and weakness. We are going to dive deeper into this in future chapters, but for now write down as many as you can think of in each category. Ask a trusted advisor if you can't list more than ten of each.

Before maximizing your strengths and making your weaknesses irrelevant, you must review your weaknesses. In your role as a leader, which of those weaknesses could you rely on others around you to complement? Which of those weaknesses are ones you cannot delegate to others? The latter weaknesses are ones you should attempt to gain proficiency in at the least, and perhaps even mastery.

Say, for example, you aspire to executive leadership. As you list your weaknesses, you have listed public speaking among them because you are uncomfortable presenting to a group, perhaps even a group of your peers. You stammer or stutter due to nervousness. Even the thought of standing in front of a group to share your thoughts makes your palms sweaty.

As a leader of a division, could you delegate board presentations to one of your direct reports? How about communicating your vision to your department or your company? Could someone else present your vision and have it be so compelling that those in your department would rally around you and follow you? No. I dare say the board, your department, and your company would be embracing and following your surrogate.

Review your list of weaknesses. Think about each one. Think about what you are trying to achieve with your career. Will that weakness be a liability? Can you mitigate that weakness by hiring someone on your team who is strong in that area? What if you were able to improve that area of weakness through training or study—would that impact your career in a positive way?

This time of transition is a perfect time to hone your strengths. It is also a perfect time to work on your weaknesses. You may discover that what you thought was a weakness, once developed, is a strength. You many never become a great orator, but knowing you can convey your thoughts and ideas to others will increase your confidence and make your strengths stand out even more.

Transition Journal
In your Transition Journal, reflect on your lists of strengths and weakness. Write a plan to work on the weaknesses. Write a commitment to yourself to carry out the plan.

Trust me, this works. When you read your own commitment later, you will hold yourself accountable!

2

What's Your Sign?

No, I'm not talking about your zodiac sign. I'm talking about your brand. No, I'm not talking about the mark you burn on your livestock to identify them (if you are reading this book, chances are great you are not a rancher). I'm talking about your personal brand. I'm talking about your personal reputation and the impression people have of you. What do you mean, you don't have a personal brand? Of course you do. Everyone does. You have a reputation. People have an impression of you. The question is, is it intentional? Is it a brand you have cultivated? Is it a brand that represents you? Please know that a brand is not a façade. Your brand must be genuine. Also, you can only have one brand. It is not possible to maintain a personal life brand and a professional life brand. Social media blew that up years ago. Trust me, those pictures you posted of that party in college are part of your permanent record.

Here is another exercise for you. Call up a friend, someone who you trust to give honest feedback. Have them look you up on LinkedIn. Ask them to describe you based on what they see. What impression do they have based solely on your LinkedIn profile? (Of course, you could ask some stranger to do this, but they will probably think you're weird.) How would they describe your reputation based on your profile? Have them repeat this process on Facebook, Instagram, and Twitter.

Next (and you can do this one yourself, though a third party can give you an unbiased view), go to Google. Yes, we are going to get our Google on. Google yourself. Yes, seriously! Come on, you know you've done it before. Just do it. You may need to do this a couple of times. For example, I would search on Jeffrey S. Ton, Jeffrey Ton, and Jeff Ton to get a full picture. How many entries about you are there on page one? What do they say about you? What impression do they give?

Why do this exercise? Because any recruiter, talent acquisition professional, or HR professional is going to do this before you get interview number one.

Why all this talk about brands, you ask? Because you are now in sales. You are selling *you*. *You* are the product; *you* are the brand. You want an organization to hire (buy) you. They must see you in your brand. They must see what is in it for them should they hire you. They have a problem. *You* are the solution.

Let's spend some time defining your brand.

Four components make up your personal brand: strengths, values, passions, and purpose. We will review each one using a three-step process. Step one is self-reflection. In this step you will answer a series of questions in your journal. Next, take an assessment that measures the component (if you are working with a coach, please follow their recommendations). In the third step, you will ask for feedback from those who know you.

Strengths

The key here is to know and understand your strengths. The goal will be to list your top five strengths. You've done a little bit of this work in chapter 1.

Self-Reflection

In your journal, answer the following questions:

- Thinking back on your career, which two or three projects you were a part of were most successful?
- For each of those projects, think about your contributions. What were the key skills or talents you used in that contribution?
- Over your career, you have held many roles—not necessarily titles, but roles. For example, your title might have been lab manager, but your role was construction materials quality assurance engineer. Which roles stand out? Why?
- Reflect on your personal and professional life. What were the most significant challenges you have been able to overcome? What skills or talents did you use to overcome them?

Now that you have written these answers in your journal, pause and reflect on your answers (and keep writing in your journal). Were there common themes? Common strengths or tactics you used? Are there specific ones you enjoy exercising more than others? How about some that you hope to never have to do again? Are there some you wish you could do better?

What of weaknesses? Are there some you overcame with some degree of success? Which skills were best left to other people on the projects? Which ones would have impacted the project positively if you had been able to perform them yourself?

We are going to start building your Personal Brand Amplifier. Visit www.JeffreySTon.com/AYJS/Resources to download a copy today. Alternatively, you could draw something like this in your journal:

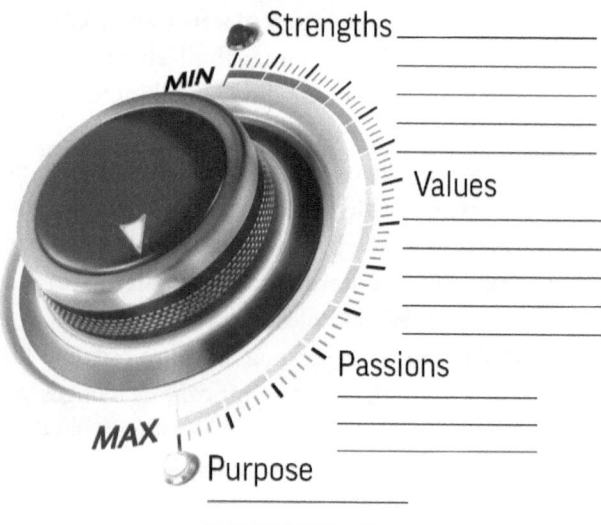

Around the dial you will notice major "clicks" and minor "clicks" representing amping up the brand. Each major click is labeled with one of the four components of your personal brand: strengths, values, passions, purpose.

Next to the minor clicks under "Strengths," write your top five strengths beside each click.

Assessment

If you have taken an assessment that helps to identify your strengths and weaknesses (and you can put your hands on it), refer to it now. If you have not taken an assessment or you cannot find the results of one you have taken, now is the time to take a strengths and weaknesses assessment. The PAIRIN Mindset assessment is a great way to determine your soft skills and mindset (it is also free as part of the offer I will let you in on at the end of this chapter). Another assessment I like is CliftonStrengths, formerly known as StrengthFinders 2.0 (there is a fee associated with taking this assessment). There is a link in the Resources section at the back of this book. Your coach may have one they prefer.

Once you have completed the assessment, I highly recommend paying the fee to obtain a readout from a coach to help you understand the results.

After completing the assessment and the readout, compare the results with the strengths you listed in your Personal Brand Amplifier. Were there similarities? Were there some surprises? Make any changes you feel compelled to make to your Personal Brand Amplifier. Be sure to write in your journal what changes you made and why.

Feedback

Seeking feedback is sometimes the hardest thing we can do as humans. We are being vulnerable. We may receive feedback we don't like or with which we disagree. Tough! You need to do it anyway. This will be some of the most valuable feedback you receive in your career.

For this step, I recommend using a survey tool like SurveyMonkey. You could, of course, use email, but be ready for wide variances in the response you get back. You are going to write a one-question survey:

> If you were to describe my key strengths, which THREE of the following would you use? (There are blanks for you to use your own words to describe my strengths if needed.)

As options under this question list your five strengths, some of the weaknesses you would like to work on, and some other attributes you would use to describe yourself. Make sure you have at least ten to choose from. Provide three spaces for them to add their own terms.

Write an email to the connections you would like to complete the survey asking them for their help, thanking them in advance and giving them a deadline for the responses. Your email could read something like this:

> Dear Jackie,
>
> I hope this email finds you well!
>
> As you may have heard, I am in transition from Acme. As I begin my search for my dream job, I am taking some time to reflect upon my career, my skills, and my passions.
>
> I value your insights and opinion. Would you be willing to complete a one-question survey? Yes, only one question! Please click on the link below to take the anonymous one-question survey. It

would be helpful if you would complete the survey by Friday at 3 p.m.

[put the survey link here]

Thank you in advance for your participation and your candor.

Sincerely,

James

Send this email to a minimum of twenty people. They should be people you know well and who are likely to complete the survey. Think about former managers, coworkers, employees, friends, family (make sure they will be truthful and candid with you), people from your church, and others with whom you have a good relationship. Don't hesitate to send it to that coworker with whom you didn't always agree; you might be surprised at the valuable feedback.

After the deadline for the survey responses has passed (don't forget to send a reminder or two), run a report to compile the results. Compare the results with those in your Personal Brand Amplifier. Make any necessary changes and, of course, capture your reasons in your Transition Journal.

Values

We are now going to repeat that process of self-reflection, assessment, and feedback for your values.

Your values are what guide you. They are your compass. They point you to what is good and beneficial. They identify what is important or useful to you. They describe what is beautiful, desirable, and constructive. They guide our behavior and influence our choices.

Values can be hard to define at times. Many times, values are easier to identify when you are involved in a situation that runs counter to your values.

Self-Reflection

Think about different organizations or projects over your career. When did you feel discord? Was it because you disagreed with the direction or because it went against your values? We have all been part of a project in which some number of people seemed to do all the work. Others appeared to be coasting. How did you feel? Did it bother you? Perhaps it is because you value hard work, integrity, and truthfulness.

Perhaps an organization you worked for made a mistake. Instead of owning up to the mistake with its customers and stakeholders, the company chose to hide it. That discomfort you felt in the pit of your stomach was a misalignment of values.

In your Transition Journal, write a few stories that come to mind. Of course, you can write of times when your values were aligned with those around you as well. Look for themes and similarities in the stories.

"Your Values Worksheet" gives a list of values. Review the list and put a check by those that align with you. Cross out those that do not apply. (You can download a copy from www.JeffreySTon.com/AYJS/Resources instead of writing in your book!) Review the values with checkmarks. Pick the five that you feel most describe you.

On your Personal Brand Amplifier, under "Values,"

YOUR VALUES WORKSHEET

Objective: Narrow this list to five values to which you relate the most.

Accessibility	Courage	Empathy	Calmness
Honesty	Originality	Speed	Love
Accomplishment	Creativity	Enthusiasm	Discipline
Humor	Passion	Spirituality	Sensitivity
Accountability	Curiosity	Excellence	Growth
Imagination	Peace	Spontaneity	Charity
Accuracy	Dependability	Experience	Optimism
Impact	Perfection	Stability	Control
Adventure	Determination	Expertise	Respect
Independence	Power	Strength	Directness
Affection	Clarity	Fairness	Security
Integrity	Prosperity	Success	Grace
Affluence	Comfort	Faith	Challenge
Intelligence	Punctuality	Sympathy	Mindfulness
Altruism	Commitment	Fame	Efficiency
Justice	Recognition	Teamwork	Sincerity
Ambition	Compassion	Family	Generosity
Kindness	Relaxation	Understanding	Celebrity
Assertiveness	Completion	Fidelity	Loyalty

write your five values next to the minor clicks. Many times, the definition of a value word could be ambiguous (e.g., what I think is a challenge might not be a challenge to you). For each value word you wrote on the Amplifier, in your journal, write one or two sentences that define the value for you (e.g., "Challenge: I like assignments that challenge me mentally to either solve a puzzle or learn something new").

Assessment

Like you did for your strengths, you need to take an assessment that helps to identify your values. You may have taken one in the past. If you can locate it, you can use it here. However, if you took it more than a year ago, consider taking it again. To dig a little deeper on your values, I like the Personal Values Assessment from Barrett Values Centre. Your coach may have one they prefer.

I highly recommend paying an extra fee to the assessment company to have a specialist perform a readout with you. If you are using a coach, they can provide this as well.

After completing the assessment and the readout, compare the results with the values you listed in your Personal Brand Amplifier. Were there similarities? Were there some surprises? Make any changes you feel compelled to make to your Personal Brand Amplifier (be sure to write in your journal what changes you made and why).

Feedback

It's time once again for the dreaded feedback! But, before we do that, we have a journaling exercise to do. Reflect on the value stories you wrote in your journal. What actions could you have taken to ensure you were acting within your value structure? What steps can you take now to ensure you are act within your value structure in the future? Finished? Now, it's time for that feedback.

We are going to revisit SurveyMonkey (or another survey tool) for this step. Once again, you are going to write a one-question survey:

> If you were to describe my values, which THREE of the following would you use? (There are blanks for you to use your own words to describe my values if needed.)

As options under this question list your five values and at least five more that were close seconds. Make sure you have at least ten to choose from. Provide three spaces for them to add their own terms.

Using the template we used for your strengths, write an email asking the recipient to complete a one-question survey.

Send this email to a minimum of twenty people. It could be the same twenty you used before, but it doesn't have to be. If you opt to use some of the same people for these exercises, consider combining the surveys into one three-question survey (and adjust the text of your email accordingly).

After the deadline for the survey responses has passed, run a report to compile the results. Compare the results with those in your Personal Brand Amplifier. Make any necessary changes and capture your reasons in your Transition Journal.

Passions

Lather, rinse, repeat. Let's repeat the process of self-reflection, assessment, and feedback to identify your passions.

Let's talk about your passions—you know, things that are your jam. Things that get you jazzed up. Things that when you talk about them, your face lights up, your voice gets that added inflection, and your body language screams "I *love* this!" What are those things? Write them down (you knew that was coming by now, didn't you?).

Self-Reflection

In your Transition Journal, write down what things about your job really get your juices flowing. Outside of work, what things do you undertake that get you so excited you can't wait to do them and tell someone about them? If you just won the lottery, and earning an income was no longer an obstacle, what would you do tomorrow? (And don't tell me, "I'd go to work tomorrow." I'm not buying what you're selling!)

Ask yourself (and write the answers): What things do you like to read? What movies or TV shows are you drawn to watch? Don't worry, the question isn't "what can I make money doing?"—yet. For now, the key is to find two or three things that light your fire.

By now, you should have a list of three or four, perhaps more. If you are struggling, try to come up with two. In your journal, reflect upon your answers. Are there common themes? Dig beneath the surface. What is it about that pursuit that fuels your passion?

Let me give you an example. I love the story of Lewis and Clark. I could talk for hours about their expedition. Ask anybody who knows me. I light up when I talk about them. The thing is, I hated history as a kid. So, it is not about history, per se. I also like genealogy, antiques (with a personal provenance), and visiting the places of my ancestors (and of Lewis and Clark). What is the common thread woven through that fabric? Stories. I love the stories of the past. What were people thinking, feeling, experiencing? I love it when a story comes alive. Understanding that helps me understand my life and the lives of those around me. I have found, in the most unlikely way, I love telling stories. *That* is one of my passions, that and the Rolling Stones, music in general, canoeing…but those are stories for another day.

The next major click of your Personal Brand Amplifier is passions. Next to the minor clicks under "Passions," add two or three of your passions.

Assessment

After self-reflection, it is time to take another assessment (of course, if you have a recent assessment, you can use those results). There are several assessments that help identify your passions, I like the Passion Test from GeniusU. Your coach may have one they prefer.

After the assessment, you will want to have a readout from your coach or other person trained in that assessment.

After completing the assessment and the readout, compare the results with the passions you listed in your Personal Brand Amplifier. Were there similarities? Were there some surprises? Make any changes you feel compelled to make to your Personal Brand Amplifier. Be sure to write in your journal what changes you made and why.

Feedback

Yes! More feedback!

Back to SurveyMonkey. You are going to write a one-question survey:

> If you were to describe my passions, which THREE of the following would you use? (There are blanks for you to use your own words to describe my passions if needed.)

As options under this question list your passions and at least seven more that were close seconds. Make sure you have at least ten to choose from. Provide three spaces for them to add their own terms.

Compose an email similar to the ones you have used for strengths and values.

Send this email to a minimum of twenty people.

After the deadline for the survey responses has passed (don't forget to send a reminder or two), run a report to compile the results. Compare the results with those in your Personal Brand Amplifier. Make any necessary changes and capture your reasons in your Transition Journal.

By now, you are asking yourself, why couldn't I just send one survey and get the feedback all at once? You could. But I've found that people are more inclined to answer one question rather than three or four. They take more time and are more thoughtful. However, if you have concern over emailing the same people three or four times, combine the first three steps into one survey. The idea is to get the most thoughtful responses to your survey.

Purpose

The final step into understanding your personal brand is to identify your purpose. (Haven't you always wanted to know your purpose in life, anyway?) But what is a purpose anyway? The Oxford dictionary defines purpose as "the reason for which something is done or created or for which something exists." John Qualls, CEO of Purpose HQ, defines purpose this way: "Your purpose is using your talent and skills to solve a problem people care about and need the solution, and you are rewarded for it."

Self-Reflection

Read back over your Transition Journal thus far. You have identified your strengths, values, and passions. In your journal, list your talents and your skills. What problems do you like to solve? (Don't worry about the reward part just yet.) Think back over the last five years. What problems have you solved? Which solutions involved leveraging your strengths, values, and passions?

Put yourself five years into the future. Imagine the world five years from now. Close your eyes and picture it. What does your family look like? Larger? Smaller? Who is married? Who is divorced? What job are you in? What industry? What does that industry look like five years from now? Since this is a book about finding a job, what does your resume look like in five years? What new entries? What new skills? What problems have you solved?

Think even further into the future. You are retiring. You are at your retirement party. There is cake, ice cream, perhaps an adult beverage or two. What are people saying about you? Looking back, what are you most proud of in your career? What problems did you solve?

Read back over what you have written (you are writing this in your Transition Journal, right?). Which of the problems that you solved related to your passions? Which ones aligned with your values? Which ones used the most of your strengths? Pick one. On your Personal Brand Amplifier under "Purpose," list no more than two purposes you identified next to the clicks.

Assessment

It is possible you have already taken an assessment to help you identify your purpose. Refer to it now. If you have not taken an assessment or you cannot find the results of one you have taken, now is the time to take a purpose assessment. Identifying your purpose can be a journey. There are several assessments that can help you identify the types of activities that bring a feeling of purpose to your life. At the end of this chapter is an offer to access

Purpose HQ. This site provides access to six different assessments that when used together can help you identify your purpose. For a single assessment, I prefer Sparketype from the Good Life Project. Your coach may have one they prefer.

After completing the assessment and the readout, compare the results with the purpose you listed in your Personal Brand Amplifier. Were there similarities? Were there some surprises? Make any changes you feel compelled to make to your Personal Brand Amplifier. Be sure to write in your journal what changes you made and why.

Feedback

At this point in the process, you should have completed your Personal Brand Amplifier. Now is the time to ask for feedback on the entire Personal Brand Amplifier. Download the PDF at www.JeffreySTon.com/AYJS/Resources and transfer your clicks from your journal or working copy of your Personal Brand Amplifier.

Using SurveyMonkey, create a one-question survey:

> Attached is a copy of my Personal Brand Amplifier. Please select a number between 1 and 10 to indicate how well I am represented by the Amplifier. 1 indicates this does not represent me at all. A 10 indicates this is a perfect representation of the me you know.

Include a freeform text box with the prompt:

> Please write in any comments you have that further clarify your answer.

Write an email to the connections you would like to provide you with feedback asking them for their help, thanking them in advance, and giving them a deadline for the responses.

Send this email to a minimum of twenty people. Don't forget to attach your Personal Brand Amplifier!

After the deadline for the survey responses has passed (don't forget to send a reminder or two), run a report to compile the results. Compare the results with those in your Personal Brand Amplifier. Make any changes and capture your reasons in your Transition Journal.

Personal Brand Amplifier

Print a copy of your completed Personal Brand Amplifier and place it in a spot where you will see it. It will serve as your guide for the remainder of this journey (and beyond).

Coaches

Throughout this chapter and the remainder of this book, I mention coaches. You are on one of the most important journeys in your life. Wouldn't it be great to have a guide? A coach is just that: a guide. They will serve as an interpreter of the results of this chapter. They will serve as an accountability partner in the waters ahead. They will be a sounding board for ideas. They will provide insights along the way.

Can you make this journey without one? Certainly. Will the journey be harder without one? Absolutely. Will the job you land be your dream job, the one that aligns with your strengths, values, passions, and purpose? Maybe. Maybe not. There are no guarantees. But wouldn't you want to take advantage of all the resources to stack the deck in your favor?

Reflection

At the end of each chapter, you will spend time with your Transition Journal. The personal journey of discovery you have been on in this chapter required some intense journaling. Read back over your entries. What did you learn about yourself? What changed during these exercises? How do you feel about the journey ahead?

About That Offer

Earlier in this chapter, I mentioned an offer that would help you manage the various assessments you have taken and those that you will take as a part of this journey. What if I told you there was an app for that? Purpose HQ is just that. It is a software-as-a-service app that provides a document repository for your assessment results, access to six different assessments (four free and two with nominal fees), and access to trained coaches to help you interpret those results. Now what if I told you that you can have access to Purpose HQ for *free*? You would jump at the offer, wouldn't you? Well, it's true. This offer includes access to the platform to store all your assessment results and four free assessments. (Fees apply for two optional assessments and optional coaching.) To take advantage of this offer, send me an email at Jeff.Ton@TonEnterprisesLLC.com and ask for Purpose HQ access.

3

You've Accomplished a Lot!

So, is now the time to dust off the resume? No, not yet. We are going to use your resume in this chapter. But we aren't ready to update it just yet.

You've done a lot in your career. You've learned some great lessons. You've accomplished some great things. Can you remember them all? Now is the time to try! In this chapter you will build a list of your accomplishments, refine that list, and begin to prepare a subset of the list for your—you guessed it—resume!

This process will take some time and thought, even though you have done some of this work in the first two chapters (you did do the work, right?). As you review your strengths, values, passions, and purpose, it will jog memories of specific companies, volunteer organizations, and social clubs you have been involved with throughout your career.

Making a List and Checking It Twice

No, this is not your naughty and nice list; this is a list of all the organizations you have been associated with since leaving high school—yes, high school. In your Transition Journal, write a career timeline.

Write down the year you graduated from high school.

Did you have a summer job between graduation and college? Write that down.

Where did you go to college? What years? Write that down.

Add a list of the organizations you were associated with during those years: fraternity, sorority, campus organizations, church organizations, clubs you belonged to, and summer jobs, internships, jobs during the academic year.

Perhaps, after high school, you went into the military. Write that down. Where did you train? Where did you serve? What years? After the military, did you go to college? Write down your college history as well.

Did you graduate from college? What year? Did you go on to pursue an advanced degree? Write it down.

What was your first job out of college? What years? Begin to build a timeline of the companies you worked for and when. What titles and/or roles did you hold while there?

Add a list of the organizations you were associated with during those years: volunteer organizations, side jobs, church organizations, board positions. Try to think of them all.

Continue the process of listing company, title or role, years, and outside organizations. Use prior versions of your resume to jog your memory. List any part-time jobs you held to supplement your income.

If you have a gap in your timeline, add some notes that describe what you were doing. Perhaps you took time off to raise a family; perhaps you were between jobs; maybe it was a sabbatical to travel. Be sure to list the organizations you were associated with during these times as well.

Who Do You Know?

By now, you should have a comprehensive list of all the organizations you have been associated with throughout your career. Don't worry if you have forgotten some along the way. You can always add those later.

Go back through the list. Write down the names of as many people in those organizations you can remember. Who was that kid you hung out with in college? What were the names of your superiors in the service? Who were your bosses, your coworkers? If you were a den mother for Cub Scouts, what were the names of the other adults? If you sat on a board for your church, who else was on that board?

As your list of names grows, think about how many of them you are connected with today. Are you friends on Facebook? How about LinkedIn? Remember those connections you used to get feedback from in chapter 2? How are you connected to them? Where do they align with your timeline?

We are going to talk a lot about how to leverage social media platforms in your job search later in this book. For now, identify the people in your list that you are currently connected with. If you aren't connected with someone, spend some time and try to connect on LinkedIn and whatever other social networks you are active on. Your network will be the most powerful aspect of your search. Take the time now to build upon it!

What Did You Do?

It is time to get a bit more formal. To this point, you have been using your Transition Journal to write your timeline. Download the Accomplishment Amplifier from www.JeffreySTon.com/AYJS/Resources. You could, of course, create your own similar to the one shown, but where would the fun be in that?

Transfer your career timeline from your Transition Journal to the Accomplishment Amplifier. Try to keep your jobs in chronological order as best you can. Use the Start Date column to maintain the order. Of course, if you're using a spreadsheet, you can always just sort on this column later.

Once you have transferred your list, start at the first row. Under the Responsibilities column, add a few sentences or bullet points to describe the responsibilities you had while in that role. Be as specific as you can, but if you can't remember all the details, that is okay. You will be coming back to this list, and you can add more details as you recall them.

As you are filling in the responsibilities, if an accomplishment occurs to you, go ahead and add that under the Accomplishments column. Don't focus on trying to fill out both responsibilities and accomplishments; just capture them as they occur to you.

Now that you have responsibilities for each role, start back at the top and add accomplishments under that column. Don't confuse responsibilities with accomplishments. Responsibilities are the definition of the work that needs to be done. Accomplishments are what you achieved while living up to your responsibilities. They are both measurable and unique to you and your experience in

YOU'VE ACCOMPLISHED A LOT!

ACCOMPLISHMENT AMPLIFIER

START DATE	END DATE	COMPANY / ORGANIZATION	ROLE/TITLE	RESPONSIBILITIES	ACCOMPLISHMENTS	PROBLEM	ACTION	RESULTS

that role. For example, note the difference between "Was responsible for an IT team of 25 FTEs" and "Oversaw a team of 25 IT professionals and successfully implemented programs to achieve the service level objectives two consecutive years." Try to list at least three accomplishments for each role. It's okay to use bullet points. Be as detailed as you can, however. If the details are a bit fuzzy, you can add them later.

Accomplishments can sometimes be difficult to recall. Ask yourself a series of questions relevant to the organization listed. Did you save the organization money? Did you make a process more efficient? Did you identify a new revenue stream? Increase quality? Increase sales? Introduce new technology?

And what of yourself? What promotions did you receive? What recognition did you earn? What new skill did you learn? What goals did you achieve? What special committees were you on? Did you lead or contribute to any special projects?

And what of the people? Did you build an exceptional team? Make a great hire? Develop your team or individuals? Develop a team member to backfill your role? What of your peers? What were they able to accomplish through your support?

Don't try to do all this in one sitting. Take your time. Make the list. Add responsibilities. Add accomplishments. Pause between the steps. Pause for an hour. Pause for a day. Come back and add more. Review the list. Add other details that occur to you.

Pause

After you have spent several days with your list, push the Pause button. Seriously. Set aside an hour. Look back over your Accomplishment Amplifier. Reflect on the list. You have accomplished a lot. You have accomplished some great things. You have impacted hundreds of lives. Be proud. Be confident. Let your mind remember. Remember the people. Remember the stories. Remember how good it felt when you accomplished an item on your list. Don't write. Don't journal. Just reflect.

After pausing for an hour, look back over your Accomplishment Amplifier. Write down details, accomplishments, and responsibilities that occurred to you during your pause. Don't worry if you don't remember everything from your reflection.

Memory Jogger: Let's Do Coffee

If you are like me, you will need a memory jogger (or two, or three). If you have some gaps in your Accomplishment Amplifier, reach out to one or two of your connections from that time period. Invite them to coffee (or tea, lunch, a beer, a phone call, or a Zoom call). Spend some time reminiscing. Tell stories. Listen to stories. If you feel comfortable, tell them you want to take notes; if not, be sure to write your notes as soon after the conversation as possible.

Go back to your Accomplishment Amplifier and fill in the details from your notes. Have as many coffee meetings as it takes to have at least three accomplishments for every role. Have more coffees if you'd like. Building a strong, vibrant network is what this book is all about!

Feedback

Time for more coffee! Now is the time to share your Accomplishment Amplifier. Share it with your coach, a mentor, your spouse, a friend, or all of the above. Invite them to coffee. Review the list with them. Invite them to ask questions. As they ask questions about a role, or organization, or time, tell stories. Tell them about the people, the organization, the accomplishments. Have three or four in mind that you would like to tell them about. If they don't ask about those specific roles, bring them up. Tell stories.

Remember the questions they ask during your stories. Write those questions and answers down. Remember their reactions. Were they as excited about your stories of accomplishment as you were? Did they understand why that specific accomplishment was important? Did they understand the impact? Take note of those as well; you may need to hone your story.

Between these coffee meetings, review your Accomplishment Amplifier. Add notes and details from your conversations. Refer to your Personal Brand Amplifier. Do the accomplishments underscore your strengths, values, passions, and purpose? Which of your stories were more compelling? Why? Did they align more with your Personal Brand Amplifier? Did you learn something through this process that compels you to modify the Personal Brand Amplifier? Update it. It's okay; it's *your* personal brand!

Writing the Stories

"Wait! I'm not an author! I'm not a writer! I can't tell stories."

Yes! You can do this. You can tell your stories. I'm going to teach you an easy formula to follow.

Think about any movie you have watched or any novel you have read. They follow the same basic formula of characters, setting, plot, conflict, and resolution.

Characters—that's easy. That's you! Okay, it's also your peers, boss, and other coworkers, but you get the point. You are the hero of the story. Hey! It is your accomplishment, it will be your resume, and you are the product you are selling. Now, just to clarify, you are not writing a work of fiction. You had a significant contribution to making this happen, right?

Setting—that's easy, too. It's the company or organization you were with at that time. Think of the office, or plant, or other physical surroundings. Think of the time, the context of the story. Was it the 1990s, 2000s, later? What was going on at the time within the company? The industry? The economy?

Plot—that's the problem. No, the plot is not a problem, the plot is *the* problem you were trying to solve. You accomplished something, right? Why were you doing it? That's the plot of your story.

Conflict—that's the challenge. What did you overcome to be successful? If it were easy, anybody could have done it, but you did it. What were the obstacles and roadblocks? What stood in the way of success?

Resolution—this is your "and they lived happily ever after" moment. What did you do to overcome the challenge? How were you successful? And—this is important—what were the results? Yes, it's your accomplishment, but what did that accomplishment mean to the organization or the people? Why should your listener care about the accomplishment?

See? Easy peasy!

Let's look at an example. In your Accomplishment Amplifier you have listed what is shown in the figure.

Here's the story:

In 2010, I was hired to be the CIO for a leading nonprofit organization. In 2010, the country was still recovering from the financial collapse of 2008–2009. Nonprofits were being called upon to stretch their capabilities. Forward-thinking CEOs knew in order to stay viable and, more importantly, to grow, they would need to leverage technology in ways they had never considered. My first order of business was to guide the team of twenty-five IT professionals in the development of a strategic plan.

Not only had the organization never had an IT strategic plan, but no one on the team had ever been involved in developing one. In addition, the leadership team would need to be convinced of IT's strategic value to the company and to invest in the strategy.

Using a combination of teaching (both with the team and the leadership), influence, and negotiation, we were able to develop a comprehensive five-year plan. The plan was written in a business-first approach as opposed to a technology-first approach. It was in the language of the business. It told the story and painted a picture of the future.

The plan was adopted unanimously by the leadership team and the board of directors. A year into execution the board wanted third-party validation of the plan (considering the investments they were making). A prestigious consulting firm was brought in to review the

YOU'VE ACCOMPLISHED A LOT!

ACCOMPLISHMENT AMPLIFIER

START DATE	END DATE	COMPANY / ORGANIZATION	ROLE/TITLE	RESPONSIBILITIES	ACCOMPLISHMENTS	PROBLEM	ACTION	RESULTS
5/1/2010	10/1/2015	Save the World Organization	Chief Information Officer	Develop Technology Strategic Plan	Defined and Implemented 5-year Strategic Plan			

plan and our current state. They validated the plan with no significant recommendations.

Over the five years of the plan we were able to execute it and realize the vision of what we set out to build. Our tagline, "Any device, any time, any place," became a reality, enabling the business to increase its revenues by 25 percent, while at the same time decreasing its technology spend as a percentage of revenue by 0.5 percent. From a mission perspective, the organization grew by several thousand employees, expanded its educational programs by several thousand participants, and added new services to its portfolio.

This story could easily be expanded to provide more detail. As you relate it, if the listener is particularly engaged with the story, dig deeper. Explain the level of resistance you met from the leadership team. Talk in detail about the techniques you used to teach and grow the staff throughout the process. Give specific ways you realized the vision of the strategic plan.

Remember, you are not going to go into this level of effort on each accomplishment. Just the ones you get asked about in your coffee meetings or the ones you choose to highlight your story, your brand, and your career.

Now it's time to hone your stories and have some more coffee. Take your Accomplishment Amplifier and meet with a few more people from your network or, perhaps even better, new additions to your network. Share the Accomplishment Amplifier with them and tell your stories. Take notes and be sure to update your Accomplishment Amplifier and your Personal Brand Amplifier.

By now, you should have a set of accomplishments and stories that paint a picture of your career for anyone with whom you meet. The picture should align with your personal brand, it should differentiate you as you, and it will stand out among the competition.

It's time to take that first step toward writing your resume. Yes, really!

PAR: It's Not Just for Golf

In his book *The Executive Job Search: A Comprehensive Handbook for Seasoned Professionals*, author Orrin G. Wood describes a tool to begin to turn your list of accomplishments into resume-ready items.

The first step is to perform a PAR analysis on your most meaningful accomplishments. PAR stands for problem, actions, and results. For each of the accomplishments in your Accomplishment Amplifier, complete the final three columns: Problem, Actions, Results. What was the problem you or the organization faced? What actions did you take to solve the problem? What were the results after the problem was solved? Huh! Almost like telling a story, isn't it?

For those accomplishments that stand out as significant in your career (i.e. they align with your Personal Brand Amplifier, raise the most interest in your conversations, or, in later steps, are germane to a job to which you are applying), perform a PAR analysis. This is a one-page analysis for each significant accomplishment. It includes:

> **Problem:** Describe the problem in two or three sentences.
>
> **Actions:** Describe the actions taken to resolve

the problem. Each action should be a sentence or two.

Results: List the results.

Resume Bullet: Write the accomplishment as it will appear on your resume.

Skills Used: List all the skills you used to solve the problem.

Using my example above the PAR would look like this:

Problem: Organization wanted to grow, and to do that, it needed a technology strategy that aligned with their business objectives. Team was inexperienced in developing a strategy.

Actions:
- Divided the process into sections. First section was focused on discovery. Second section was on education and training (the "why").
- Personally chaired each committee to help guide and teach.
- Began to meet with executive staff to build relationships and educate.
- As the plan developed provided updates to all stakeholders.
- Presented the final plan and negotiated the budget.

Results:
- Business grew revenue by 25 percent.

- Costs as a percentage of revenue decreased by 0.5 percent.
- Mission services added; expanded reach by several thousand people.

Resume Bullet: ? (see below)

Skills Used: Presentation skills, teaching, coaching, negotiation, planning, creativity, collaboration, systems thinking, foresight

Turning your PAR into a resume bullet can be challenging. Your coach, a recruiter, or an HR professional can provide guidance; however, you should take a crack or two at each one and then get feedback. Here are some tips you can use to build the resume bullets:

- Start each one with an action verb.
- Provide tangible results where you can. Dollars, percentages, and numbers help the reader see the impact. If you don't have specific results, always underestimate the result; never overestimate.
- Don't use jargon or acronyms.
- Use only a sentence or two.
- Describe the obstacles or challenges you overcame. Remember your story!

Continuing the example:

Resume Bullet: Defined and implemented a strategy for technology and marketing to enable company to leverage its assets and customer base enabling the organization to grow by 25 percent in operating revenue while reducing costs as a percentage of revenue by 0.5 percent.

Team accomplishments are tough. But yes, you should claim them. As you are writing your resume bullet, Wood recommends adding the phrase "Played a key role in" to your bullet. Be sure you can back up the key role you played in an interview.

Reflection

You have accomplished a lot, not only in your career but also in your journey thus far. In your Transition Journal, spend some time reflecting on the exercises in chapter 3. What do you feel as you read your list of accomplishments? How has your confidence changed during the process? What did it feel like to connect with old friends and colleagues? Which ones stand out for you? Of the conversations you have had over coffee, which of those stand out? Why? Did the journey of chapter 3 validate or change your Personal Brand Amplifier? How? What did you learn about yourself?

4
It Begins and Ends with Your Network

As you may have surmised by now, I am a big proponent of networking. (For you information technology pros out there, I am not talking about the kind of networking that connects computer systems together; I am talking about the kind of networking that connects people together.) At the time of this writing, 87 percent of jobs are filled through your network (up from 43 percent ten years ago). The old adage "It's not what you know but who you know" rings truer and truer. But this is not about nepotism. This is about the value of a warm introduction that separates you from hundreds of other job seekers.

Even if you are a master networker, don't skip this chapter. You will pick up a few nuggets, and the exercises along the way will be foundational to your success in later chapters.

If the mere mention of the word *network* makes your

palms sweaty and your stomach queasy as you conjure up images of cocktail parties, corporate networking events, or the networking time at conferences, you are not alone, my friend. I was (and am) right there with you. Here is my promise from someone who started a job search with twenty connections on LinkedIn: You will not regret building a strong, vibrant network. The investment in time (and tissues for sweaty palms and Pepto-Bismol for the queasy stomach) will pay you back 1,000-fold.

When I began my job search with twenty connections on LinkedIn, I was stunned by all the people who were willing to drop everything to have coffee, jump on a phone call, provide insight…to *help*! I was reaching out to people I hadn't talked to in twenty years, and they said, "Sure, Jeff! I'll have coffee. Let's meet at the Starbucks by my office." I was reaching out to people I had never met. "Jeff, it's nice to meet you. Let's do coffee. How about Panera Bread on Meridian?"

After that experience, I promised myself two things. One, I would never ever let my network grow cold again. I had thought, *Why do I need to network? I am in my dream job. I am going to work here until I retire.* Two, whenever anyone would ask me for guidance and insight, my answer would be "Yes! Let's do coffee. I can meet you Tuesday. 7:30? Starbucks?"

I now have over 5,000 connections on LinkedIn and countless other people I know and connect with via social media, email, coffee, meetings, and yes, networking events. I should point out that this is not a numbers game. This is a quality game. I will get to that in a bit.

Oh, and yes. I found a job. I found a dream job. I found the perfect job. How did I find it? Through my network, of course. Two people I had coffee with in the prior two weeks sent me the same job description on the same day. It was my perfect job!

Before we go much further, I should clarify the phrase *dream job*. Finding your dream job does not mean it will be your *last* job. Circumstances change. You change. The company changes. Dreams change. You may use these strategies to find your dream job several times in your career. I found my dream job. *That* was three jobs ago! I used these strategies to find my next dream job, and then my next.

However, more important than finding my dream job is that the network I have built over the last decade continues to help me to grow and learn. It doesn't matter if I am attending a large gathering of peer professionals, meeting in a small group, or having coffee one-on-one, I come away with new knowledge, a fresh perspective, and insights I can use every day. Like the jelly of the month club in *National Lampoon's Christmas Vacation*, networking is the gift that keeps on giving!

Type of Networks

Now that you get the why of networking, let's talk about the types of networking, then we will get into the how. There are four primary types of networking opportunities. Over the course of this chapter we will explore how to leverage each one to help you land that perfect job.

Professional Networking Events

These are the events that send shivers down the spines of introverts worldwide (this one included). Professional networking events range from large conferences focused on your industry or profession to events specifically created to foster networking.

Conferences typically have large chunks of time set aside for networking: the coffee or snack time between sessions, evening entertainment and parties, dedicated meet-and-greet times, and meals.

Most communities have networking events created by the Chamber of Commerce, Better Business Bureau, or other associations. These events are great opportunities for expanding your network since they invite a wide cross section of professionals from various industries and professions.

At the time of this writing, the world is in the midst of the COVID-19 pandemic. Worldwide, large conferences and events have been canceled or gone virtual. There is a section at the end of this chapter on virtual networking.

Networking Groups

Networking groups fall into two major categories: groups focused on an industry or a profession and groups focused on job seekers (professionals in transition like you). The former conduct meetings aimed at educating their members and, more importantly, connecting its members. The latter groups serve a similar purpose but their educational component focuses on the job search and enhancing skills to improve your chances of success.

Most metropolitan areas have industry or professional groups for every discipline. Many areas have more than one. If you are in a smaller town or a rural area, you may need to commute to a larger town to participate in these groups. However, in a post-COVID world, many offer virtual participation, which can be just as beneficial. These groups may also offer a "member in transition" subgroup option with programming tailored to the job seeker.

Networking groups for the job seeker are also plentiful

in most cities. Many times, these groups are sponsored by, or at least meet in, churches. In these groups you will find a diverse membership and a somewhat transient membership as members find their next job and new members enter transition. Several of these groups provide experiences tailored to various types of jobs (office, trades, healthcare, etc.).

Community Networks

The broadest category of networking opportunities is under the umbrella of community or social networks. These include church groups, civic groups (like Rotary, Kiwanis, and others), and groups focused on a hobby or interest. Each of these provide the job seeker with opportunities to network and socialize with those who share a common interest, passion, or belief. Never underestimate the power of these networks in your job search.

One-on-One Networking

If you haven't done a lot of one-on-one networking, it may seem awkward at first, especially when meeting someone for the first time. However, of all the types of networking, this one will be the most valuable to your job search. You have already seen in earlier chapters the need to sit down one-on-one and share your story. Later in this chapter we will cover the how for one-on-one networking, but you may be wondering about the who.

Think through the networks above. In a model train club? Invite a fellow member out for coffee to talk about trains. Reach out to someone in your church, maybe that person you share a pew with every Sunday. Do you belong to a professional network group or a job seekers network? Reach out to someone in those groups. If you met someone at a conference and exchanged business cards, follow up with them.

By now you may be saying, *Well, I don't know if they have a job for me.* Or, you may be asking, *How do I ask someone for a job?* Here's the big secret: Networking is not about asking for a job. Networking is about listening to someone's story and telling your story—in that order. More on that later!

Social Networks

I know I said there were four types of networking opportunities and this makes five. No, I have not forgotten how to count. Online networks like Facebook, Twitter, Instagram, and others are tools to facilitate networking. They are valuable tools, so much so there is an entire chapter later in this book dedicated to getting the most out of those tools and the networking they provide.

Evaluating Your Network

Now is the time to evaluate your network. To do this, we will add to your collection of amplifiers. This one is your Network Amplifier. There is a template for your Network Amplifier at www.JeffreySTon.com/AYJS/Resources available for download. The Network Amplifier enables you to map out your network strategy.

Network Amplifier

The Network Amplifier is made up of spokes (the lines) and nodes (the circles). Take some time now to fill out your Network Amplifier.

Near the center node, write your name. Beginning with the "Events & Conferences" node, think of all the events you have attended in the last year. Write those events by

IT BEGINS AND ENDS WITH YOUR NETWORK 51

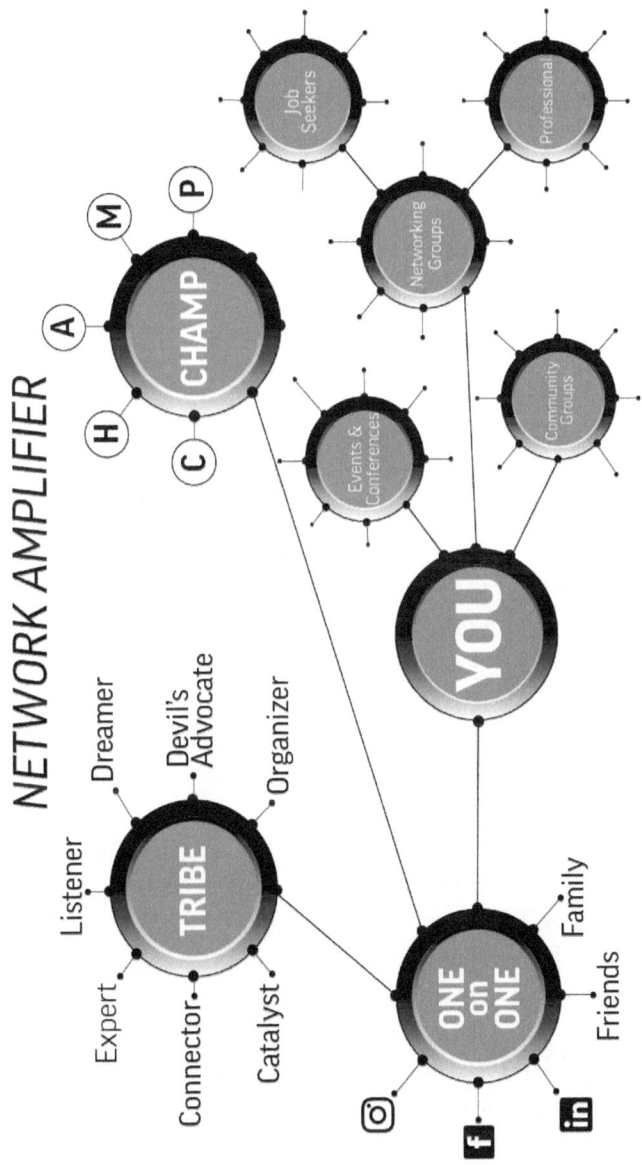

the nodes connected to "Events & Conferences." Add more spokes and nodes if needed.

Proceed to the "Networking Groups" node. How many professional or industry groups do you currently attend? Off the "Professional" node, write the names of those groups. Have you joined a job seekers group? Fill in those nodes, as well. Add more spokes and more nodes if needed.

Next up, think of the community groups with which you are involved. Write those groups by the appropriate nodes. Add additional spokes and nodes to represent all your community groups.

Finally, for the "One-on-One" node, fill in the names of everyone you know. I'm kidding! To complete this portion of the Network Amplifier, we will use numbers to represent your network. Near the "Family" node, write the number of family members with whom you have spoken with in the last year. By the "Friends" node write the number of friends you have seen or spoken with in the last six months. Next to the nodes that represent your social media connections, write the number of connections, friends, or followers you have in each. Add more spokes and nodes if you need.

Review your Network Amplifier. In your Transition Journal, reflect on your connections. Do you have a lot (by your definition)? Are there obvious gaps? What does this tell you about your level of connectedness? How does it make you feel? (Yes, there is that f-word again!)

Caution: Network Under Construction

Before turning our attention to the nuts and bolts of how to network, let's spend some time on building your network. Go back to your Network Amplifier. Where were the gaps? If you haven't attended more than one or two professional networking events in the last year, start by identifying the ones in your area. Use the search engine of your choice to find some. Talk to your peers and find out which ones they attend. Read the business section of your local paper or your local business journal. Are there trade associations for your industry or your profession? Locate their websites and look for conferences. Add the ones you find to your Network Amplifier using a different color.

Repeat this process with networking groups, both industry and job seekers groups. Ask your coach for recommendations. Reach out to peers, and ask which ones they attend and why. Add them to your Network Amplifier.

Lather, rinse, repeat for community organizations. Have a hobby or a passion? Research groups that meet to talk about it. Update your Network Amplifier.

Now that you have groups identified, it is time to talk about people. After all, networking involves person-to-person dialogue. Let's do a deeper dive into the people in your network. To accomplish this, we are going to review your person-to-person network through a couple of lenses.

Who's in Your Tribe?

Jason Barnaby, founder of Fire Starters, Inc., and the author of *Igniting the Fire Starter Within: The Secrets to Finding Your Fire, Fanning Your Flame, and Tending Your Tribe*, has developed a great resource for identifying the different types of people you need in your network. His Tribal Inventory describes seven quintessential roles everyone should have in their tribe.

Listener: Unsurprisingly, this is the person who listens. They provide an ear for your ideas, ramblings, and plans. They ask questions and they rarely, if ever, offer advice.

Dreamer: Their favorite phrase is "what if." They take your ideas and give you dozens of ideas to build upon. The bigger the ideas, the better!

Devil's Advocate: They burst bubbles. They poke holes in your dreams and your big ideas. Sounds bad, right? It's not! They serve a critical role in keeping us grounded and real. They allow us to add detail to our dreams.

Organizer: This is the list maker. They help you think through the "this before that" steps you need to take to make your dream a reality.

Catalyst: They give you a kick in the seat of the pants when you need one. They encourage you, they challenge you, and they hold you accountable. They give you the push you need to create the best version of you.

Connector: A connector's favorite phrases are "You need to meet so and so" and "You need to read this book or blog post." They love making introductions for the sake of watching the network grow. They are the lines on your Network Amplifier.

Expert: They are your guide because they've already been there. They can provide directions and insights. They won't necessarily tell you how to navigate every bend in the river, but they will be there with advice along the journey.

You can download the Tribal Inventory from FireStartersTribe.com. Scroll to the bottom, provide your name and email, and it is yours for free. It will guide you through the exercise of identifying who in your network plays which roles. Better yet, pick up a copy of his book and get the whole story!

Your tribe are those people in your life who are there for you when you need them. They are there for you, whether you know you need them or not. Spoiler alert: You need them now more than ever.

On your Network Amplifier, find the Tribe node—it's near the One-on-One node you completed earlier. Write the names of the person or people who serve in each of the seven roles of your Tribal Inventory. It's okay if you have more than one, or if one person serves multiple roles. Chances are you met with several of these people in your work in chapter 1.

In your Transition Journal, identify your gaps. What roles are missing in your network? Where do you have one person in multiple roles? What are their strengths? Perhaps their greatest value to your network is in only one role. Think about yourself and the roles you serve in others' networks. Where are your strengths? Where do you add the most value to others? What role do you play in *their* tribe?

Mirror, Mirror, on the Wall

When you think of the people in your network, what do they look like? I mean it literally: What do they look like? Do they all look the same? Do they all share a similar background, a similar belief system? Having a diverse network provides you with many benefits. A diverse network brings diversity of thought. A diverse network reveals new perspectives. A diverse network enriches your experiences. A diverse network can open doors to you that you haven't even considered yet.

I thought I was the king of networking. After all, I had been building my professional network for eight or nine years. And then I met Amy.

Amy Waninger is the founder of Lead at Any Level and the author of *Network beyond Bias: Making Diversity a Competitive Advantage for Your Career*. Amy and I met for coffee a couple of years ago. As she described her work and her passion, she literally had me drawing my network on the back of a napkin, sitting in Starbucks. It was eye-opening and changed the way I network forever.

Her book and accompanying workbook guide you through the details, and I encourage you to read it and work through the process. For our purposes, let me paint the broad strokes. You can (and should) revisit this work once you have read her book. Read on to find a special offer from Amy at the end of this section.

To begin, think about your network in terms of the acronym CHAMP. Amy had me write this vertically down the left edge of the napkin. "CHAMP," she explained, "stands for customer, hire, associate, mentor, protege." For our purposes, use the CHAMP node on your Network Amplifier.

By the C node, write the name of someone in your

network who is your customer (current, past, or prospective). This is not someone who works for the same company as you.

H stands for hire. Write the name of someone you would recommend a friend hire, someone you would stake your reputation on.

Associate is the A in CHAMP. List the name of a person in your previous (or current) organization who holds a similar role as you. If you were a vice president, this would be another vice president.

Mentors are a valuable part of your network. Do you have a mentor? Write down their name. Don't have one? This is a gap you will want to fill!

P is for protege, someone you mentor. You do mentor someone, don't you? You can learn more from mentoring someone than just about any other type of networking.

In your Transition Journal, reflect on your CHAMP network. Are there gaps? Is there someone who comes to mind who could fill the gap? Are there other names you could add? Go ahead and write them down in a different color.

Amy wasn't done with me yet. She said, "In this next part, we are going to dig a little deeper. We are going to see how diverse your network is today." I followed her instructions to write IGGNORE (with two Gs) on my napkin. Since you don't have a napkin to work with, we are going to use the CHAMP node again.

The I in IGGNORE is for industry. Look at your CHAMP nodes. Write an I next to the name of anyone who is in a different industry from the one in which you work (or most recently worked).

The first G is for generation. We live and work at a time when there are as many as five generations in the workforce. For our purposes, let's focus on four: baby boomers (born 1946–1964), generation X (born 1965–1980), millennials (1981–1996), and generation Z (born 1997–2012). Write a G next to anyone in your CHAMP nodes who is in a different generation from yours.

Next up is gender. Gender and gender identity can be a complex subject for those who have not been introduced appropriately to the topic. Amy does a masterful job in the chapter on gender identity in her book. For our purposes, we will use male, female, nonbinary (a gender identity that is neither male nor female), and transgender (a person whose gender identity differs from the gender they were assigned at birth). Think about your CHAMP nodes. Write GN next to anyone whose gender is different from your own.

The O in our exercise stands for orientation—sexual orientation. Straight, lesbian, gay, bisexual, queer, and so on. Review the names in your CHAMP network. Put an O next to the name of anyone whose orientation you know is different from your own.

The R stands for race and ethnicity. Again, focusing on your CHAMP network, do you have someone in your network who is of a different race or ethnicity from yours? Put an R next to their name.

The E in Amy's model stands for exchange—in other words, the depth of your relationship. Put an E next to anyone's name with whom you have exchanged personal stories or know them deeply, by your own definition.

Are there any letters you were not able to write down? Think about your Tribe network. Do any of those people fill the gaps in your IGGNORE exercise? Do you still have gaps? Think about the other One-on-One nodes: family, friends, etc. Does someone come to mind who represents the missing letters in your network? Write their names on your Network Amplifier along with the letter.

Amy has created an exciting offer for anyone who reads this book and wants to learn more about her work. She has agreed to provide a PDF of her full instructions for completing your CHAMP and IGGNORE diversity network. Visit www.LeadAtAnyLevel.com/amplify-offer to take advantage of the offer.

In your Transition Journal, think about the previous exercise. Where are the gaps in your network? Did the exercise make you uncomfortable? Why? Think and reflect on why a diverse network would serve you well in your career and your life.

Reflection

As you review your completed Network Amplifier, what stands out to you? Do you have a lot of connections? Are they strong connections? Are there gaps in your Tribe One-on-One network? How about in your CHAMP or IGGNORE networks? Spend some time thinking about how you can grow and strengthen your network connections.

5

The Ins and Outs of Networking

Networking does not need to be hard. We sometimes have a tendency to put too much pressure on ourselves. Panicked, we don't know what to say. We don't know how to break the ice. Throughout this chapter, I will provide some ins and outs of networking to help you gain the confidence you need to rock the networking game.

Conferences and Events

These can be very intimidating. You walk into a room and there are dozens, possibly hundreds of people. They all seem to know each other. How do you start a conversation? Strategy, that's how. Have a plan.

Here's the number one thing to keep in mind: It's not about you. Your strategy is to find as many people as you can who you can help. *Say what?* you're thinking. *I'm the one who's out of work. I'm the one who needs a job.* Yeah, and if you show up at a networking event or conference with a stack of resumes to hand out, you are not going to be successful. Remember, your focus is finding the right job, the perfect job, your dream job. You won't find that by talking about what you need.

It's about mindset. You want to learn about the people in the room. You want to learn their stories and about their jobs. They may just have your dream job (or one similar to it). How will you know if you talk about you? You want to learn how you can help them. Everyone goes to these events to get something. Why are they here? What do they need? Can you help them get it?

I have a friend who sets a goal for every conference she attends. She wants to meet at least three people and get to know them well enough to send them a meaningful book recommendation (and sometimes even the book itself) after the conference. You must have a pretty good conversation with someone to reach that point. So how do you do it?

Don't Dance with the One Who Brought You

The first rule is to forget what Shania Twain taught you about dancing with the one who brought you. That is a great rule for dating and dancing, but not so great for building a professional network. You need to leave your pack. That can be hard, because there is comfort in the group of coworkers you came with. However, if you and your coworkers or friends are cloistered together talking about this project or that project, or even talking about the latest hot TV show, chances are slim that others you don't know will try to break into your group to start a conversation.

Scan the room. You can even walk the room to get the feel for the crowd and the energy. Stand tall, walk confidently, smile. Is there anyone standing alone? Perhaps they are as nervous as you are, or even more. With groups of three or more, assess the energy. Are they having a high-energy conversation (perhaps about the latest hot movie)? That group will be hard to join, unless maybe you're the star of that movie they're talking about. You are looking for groups having conversations, but not high-energy conversations. It's going to be far easier to break into the group.

Take Time to Smell the Roses

Now you are ready. Want to make a connection quickly? Find a fellow wallflower. Someone standing alone. Walk up to them with a smile. Make eye contact. Introduce yourself—you do know your name, don't you? Ask them how they are. Okay, that was the easy one. Ask them what brings them to the event. Was it a specific speaker or topic? Was it to meet others? Do they know others attending? What do they do? Follow that up with: "I'm fascinated by people's stories. How did you decide to be an accountant?" Always, always, always ask what you can do for them. Are there introductions you can make for them?

Get in Line!

Now, you are ready to tackle a group. No? Not yet? Okay. Get in line. Yes, get in line. Get in line at the bar, the coffee, the snacks. I am always amazed by my wife. She can get in line (typically to the ladies' room) and come back with two or three new best friends—at the very least she knows their names, their spouses' names, their kids' names, where they work…You get the gist. Again, put on that smile. Walk and stand with confidence. Try to make eye contact with those around you. Nod, smile, and ask how they are doing. Ask how they are liking the event so far.

Speaking of lines, at conferences, there are always lines

entering the room for the keynote, leaving the room, entering and leaving the breakouts. Take the same approach. Smile and try to make eye contact. Nod. Ask how they liked the speaker (of course, this works best leaving the room, not entering it). Ask if they've heard the speaker before (this can work in either case).

Break into a Group

Now, let's tackle the group. Find a group of three or more who are engaged in conversation, but not too lively. Groups of two are by nature more intimate and more closed. You will probably be interrupting a conversation. It's best to avoid them.

Stand confidently and with a smile near the most open part of the group (where there is a gap between two people, look for one person turned more at angle to the main group). Don't enter the group yet. Stay three feet or so away. When someone makes eye contact—and they *will* make eye contact—nod, smile, say hello, and step into the group. Do not reach across the group to shake hands. When appropriate and without interrupting the conversation, introduce yourself to the person to your right or left. Acknowledge others in the group. Listen to the conversation. Interject into the conversation as appropriate.

Standing outside the group will feel like an eternity. If after ten seconds or so no one has made eye contact, move on to another group. Do not circle the group looking for an opening.

Pause for a moment and think about the last several paragraphs. Remember, your goal is to find a way to help people at the event. In lines, be the one to make eye contact, smile, and nod. In groups, be the one who leaves a gap or shifts to open body language. Be the one who invites others into the group with a smile, a nod, and a hello.

Let's Do Coffee

As you meet people through your event networking or through introductions from those in your network, ask them for coffee. Coffee meetings are much more informal than lunch, not to mention it's easier to drink a cup of coffee than to eat a salad or a sandwich as you talk to people. Remember, the purpose of the coffee is not to ask them for a job. The purpose is to learn more about their story, their career, their job, and their industry.

Some people find these one-on-one conversations much easier than networking events. Still others will be petrified at the thought of talking to a stranger for thirty to sixty minutes. This really is a time when you fake it until you make it. Come armed with some questions. Do some research on the person. Read their LinkedIn profile, research their company, google them. If you were introduced to them by someone else in your network, acknowledge that and ask them how they know that person. You want to know their story. You want to know a day in the life of a CIO, an accountant, a sales executive.

They of course will want to know your story. Your goal here is to listen more than you talk, but be balanced. Don't dominate the conversation, but don't answer in one or two sentences, either.

Inevitably, your job transition (or your desire to change) will come up. Never, ever say negative things about your employer or previous employer. You want to look forward, not look back. You can say something as simple as "I am exploring career options and want to learn about different industries, different roles, and different organizations." As you hone your message, you will get much more specific, especially when asked what type of role you are interested in. More on that in a subsequent chapter.

For now, here are some tips for your coffee meeting.

Preparing for the Coffee
- Schedule well in advance.
- Use a location convenient for them.
- Provide your cell phone number (and if you are creating the meeting invitation, include it in the meeting notes).
- Connect with them on LinkedIn.
- Confirm the time and location the day before.
- Do your research—even if you know them.
  - Check out their LinkedIn profile.
  - Look at their company's website and LinkedIn page.
  - Google them and their company.

The Coffee
- Dress the part (this is true even for a virtual coffee).
- Don't overdress, either—know your guest.
- Arrive five minutes early.
- Provide your bio resume (more on this in the chapter on resumes), even if you know them.
- Introduce yourself, thank them for their time, and offer to buy their coffee.
- Remind them how you came to be connected to them. For example, "I'm glad Jill introduced us. How do you know Jill?" When they are finished, tell them how you know Jill.

- Tell them why you wanted to meet. For example, "Joe, as Jill might have shared, I am in transition from XYZ Company," or "Joe, as Jill might have shared, I am contemplating a job or career change."
- Use this prompt to launch the heart of the conversation: "To that end, I am trying to talk to as many professionals such as yourself as I can. I want to learn about their career journey."
- Now, ask the other person about their job, career, and industry: "Joe, I would love to learn more about what you do for ABC Incorporated, the industry, the challenges you face, and what gets you up in the morning to head into the office…"
- Listen and take notes! You are not going to find your dream job or your dream company by reading job titles and descriptions on job boards. You are going to find it by listening to people's stories. Remember, this is not a job interview; you want to learn about them and their career. Later, you will want to review your notes and reflect on them in your Transition Journal.
- When they ask about you, be prepared. Don't give them every detail of your career, and don't rehash what they can read on your bio resume.
- If they say, "I don't have any openings" or "I don't know of any openings," respond with "That's okay. I'm here today to learn."
- If they ask, "How can I help you?," answer with "Who else should I be speaking with? Are there three or four people in your network you could introduce me to?"

- Write down the names and companies they mention.
- Close with a thank-you and an ask. Ask how you can help them.
- If they say they can't think of anything at the moment, respond with an offer to introduce them to people in your network or people you meet with during your search. Be sure to ask what makes a good connection for them.

Follow Up

- Send a thank-you email within a day of the meeting.
- Personalize it by referring to something you discussed. For example, "The point you made about the satisfaction you receive from building strong teams really resonated with me."
- If your offer to help them resulted in something specific, mention it and provide a timeline to provide it.
- Remind them of the introductions they mentioned and provide an electronic copy of your bio resume and a link to your LinkedIn profile to make the introduction easy for them.
- Give them something. No, I don't mean a gift. I mean a link to an article from their industry or related to their role, an inspirational quote that you think might be meaningful to them, a book suggestion, or a podcast recommendation.

Virtual Coffee

At the time of this writing, we are in the midst of the COVID-19 global pandemic. Most communities are on some type of shelter-in-place restrictions, limiting movement about town to essential trips. This has put a stop, for the time being, to face-to-face meetings, especially coffee meetings. This should not stop you from networking. Invite your connections (and your new connections) to a virtual coffee.

Even after the restrictions are lifted, give the option. Some people will be more cautious in their approach to face-to-face meetings than others. If you give the option, they don't have to be uncomfortable asking for a virtual meeting. Also, given busy schedules, it may be easier for your connection to meet virtually. It certainly saves on travel time.

Here are some tips for a successful virtual coffee:

- Follow the tips under "Preparing for the Coffee" in the previous section the same way you would for a coffee in the physical world.
- Send your bio resume prior to the call.
- Make sure you are in a quiet room where you will not be interrupted. This is especially important if you are meeting someone for the first time. The dogs and the kids are cute and all, but you don't want the distractions.
- Pay attention to the lighting in the room. You don't want to look like you are in a cave, nor do you want to look like you are in an interrogation room on a 1970s cop show.

- Hey! What's behind you? No, not now…When you are the call. Is it cluttered? Clean it up. Does it distract from the focus of the call (that focus is you, by the way)? Move it. Does it conflict with your personal brand? Get rid of it.
- Zoom backgrounds. One word: No. They are fun and a cool technology, but they will detract from your image, and if the lighting isn't perfect, you will look like James T. Kirk transporting to the *Enterprise* during a power glitch…You know, not all there.
- Hey, my eyes are up here! Look at the camera. Don't stare it down, but look at, like you would look in someone's eyes in a face-to-face meeting. Looking at their image on the screen is not the same thing.
- Make sure your audio and video connections are clean, crisp, and uninterrupted. Now may be the time to upgrade your internet.
- Remember that mute may not be your friend. If you can't remember to unmute yourself when talking, don't use it.
- Handle the coffee the same way you would for a face-to-face coffee, using the tips in the previous section.
- Remember to follow up just as you would after a real-world coffee meeting. Use the tips in the previous section.

Reflection

Time to pick up your Transition Journal. Review your Network Amplifier. Where are the gaps? Reflect on ways you can close those gaps. Think about times when you were comfortable in a group. What made you feel comfortable? Did you know everyone? Did someone welcome you into the group? Think about your dream job. Describe it in your journal. Do you know or have you heard of someone who has that job? What would you ask them if you had the chance?

Look over the notes you took during your coffee meetings. What resonates with you? What aligns with your Personal Brand Amplifier? What accomplishments from your Accomplishment Amplifier would solve their challenges?

Read over your Transition Journal. What thoughts occur to you now? Is there anything you would change? Do you have any new insights into your journey?

6

Your Resume (It's About Time!)

I hear you. Some of you are thinking, "It's about time we are getting to my resume. I've been itching to get it in people's hands!" Rest assured, at the end of this chapter, you will have a rockin' resume!

Still others are saying, "I've got a resume. All I have to do is update it with the most recent position, right?" If this is you, you might be tempted to skim or even skip this chapter altogether. Don't! Don't skip this chapter unless you've been in your current role less than a year and your resume is fresh. On second thought, you should read this chapter anyway—you just might learn *the* thing that sets your resume apart from the competition.

Speed Reading

Before we dive in, we are going to play a game. Ready? You now work in HR. In fact, you work in talent acquisition in HR. You are screening applications for the role of chief information officer for your information technology (IT) department. You've read the job description and know this is an executive position, reporting to the CEO. The job calls for ten or more years' experience in leadership roles related to IT. Your company uses various technologies, some of which you have heard of, most of which you have not. You have 452 resumes to review. Your vice president has asked you to provide twenty resumes to consider for an interview.

Get out your Transition Journal and your smartphone. Open the timer function on your smartphone. Set the timer to six seconds. When I say "Go," start the timer, turn the page, and read the resume. When the timer reaches zero, stop reading and turn back to this page.

Ready? Set! Go!

Welcome back. In your Transition Journal, answer the following questions:

- What was the name of the candidate?
- Do they have the experience you need?
- What was the name of their most recent employer?
- What was one of their major accomplishments?
- What skills do they have that are most relevant to the open position?
- Last but not least, which pile does the resume go into: yes or no?

The Cold, Hard Truth

The average time spent reading a resume on the first pass is six seconds. Six seconds is less time than a cowboy rides a bucking bronco. Six seconds decide the fate of the candidate. Six seconds decide *your* fate.

This is why the first five chapters of this book are so important. You must separate yourself from the pack—er, uh, the stack. That is the value of knowing your personal brand, having confidence in your accomplishments, and investing in your network. You don't want your resume to end up in the stack.

However, even given all the hard work you have put in thus far, odds are your resume will end up in the stack, because you applied through the website, a job site, or even a recruiter, or because the network connection who offered to help merely forwarded your resume to HR. Your resume must tell such a great story that in six seconds it gets placed in the yes pile for a deeper look.

Even though the average resume is read for six seconds, it is still the key that unlocks the door to your dream job. Given that pressure, you may consider using a professional resume writer. That is a great approach and one I have used in the past. If that is the path you choose, you still should read the remainder of this chapter. It will give you the knowledge to evaluate the professional you want to use.

Purpose, Revisited

In chapter 1, we talked about your purpose. Now let's talk about your resume's purpose. It may sound obvious to say, but the purpose of your resume is to get an interview. After that, it's on you. To get that interview, your resume must convince the reader you can solve their problem. To be blunt, it's about the reader, not about you. It's about WIIFT: What's in it for them?

Your resume's job is to sell you (you are, after all, the product in this transaction) in such a way the reader is

John C. Smith

123 Smith Road, Indianapolis, IN 46256
(317) 777-7777 • LinkedIn: @jcsmith2020 • myemail@gmail.com

BUSINESS LEADER

Strategic, innovative and results-oriented business visionary with 30 years executive and hands-on experience in the design and delivery of robust, high performance solutions. Proven track record in achieving exceptional results in both entrepreneurial and institutional environments that demand continuous improvement. Proven ability to drive value, benefit by solving complex business needs while managing costs and risks. Provides strategic direction to ownership, board, stockholders and other stakeholders. Experience in a variety of industries including: retail, education, non-profit, commercial real estate, consumer electronics, manufacturing, banking, insurance, warehousing and distribution, and supply chain. Committed to personal and professional learning, growth and development.

- Strategic Technology and Business Planning
- P&L Responsibility, Budgets, and Cost Control
- Organization/Management Re-engineering
- Global Staff Management
- Large Scale Vendor Contract Negotiations
- Merger and Acquisition Integration
- Enterprise Application Strategy, Architecture and Automation
- Business Process Optimization
- Strategic Analysis and Internal Consulting
- Regulatory and Compliance Management (SOX, PCI)
- Outsourcing (Off-shore and Near-shore)
- Divestiture Decoupling

PROFESSIONAL EXPERIENCE

ROADRUNNER SYSTEMS, LLC, Indianapolis, IN 2015 – Present
Senior Vice President of Product Development & Strategic Alliances Responsible for driving the company's managed service vision and strategy and the development and management of the strategic relationships with OEMs, distributors and cloud providers. Focused on the evolving IT landscape and the changing needs of customers, together with the RoadRunner team, ensures the products and services meet clients' needs and drives value in their organizations now and in the future.

- Member of the executive team with the responsibility for overall management of the company, including defining, setting and defining corporate strategy.
- Responsibility for managing industry analyst relations, strategic vendor relations, and partner relations As the firm's first product executive, defined the company's product lifecycle, strategy and roadmap
- Led cross functional corporate wide initiatives achieving organizational alignment, market strategy definition and execution, competitive strategy and execution, and operational efficiencies
- Major product launches included:
  - DRaaS Run, Ready, & Restore; market leading disaster recovery solutions
  - @JRoadRunner Portfolio v2017; analyst recognized client portal
  - Managed and Assisted Service Models; generating significant MRR growth
  - Cyber Threat Health Review; expanding DRaaS market to include data protection

SAVE THE WORLD ORGANIZATION, INC., Indianapolis, IN 2010 - 2015
Senior Vice President of Corporate Connectivity and Chief Information Officer
Joined Save The World Organization, Inc. in 2010 to provide vision and leadership in the continued development and implementation of the enterprise-wide information technology portfolio, including applications, infrastructure, security and telecommunications across the STW business units. In 2013, STW Inc. created the position of SVP of Corporate Connectivity to bring together the Marketing and Information Technology areas under single leadership providing a cohesive strategy for conducting business in the digital age.

John C. Smith – Resume

- Member of the senior executive with responsibility for defining, setting and driving corporate strategy: including opening of four new business units across a diverse set of industries.
- Defined and implemented a strategy for technology and marketing to enable company to leverage its assets and customer base enable the organization to grow by 25% in operating revenue while keeping costs in check.
- Lead a multi-departmental team in the development and launch of the organization's loyalty card program. Exceeding all one and two year goals and enabling the company to gain insights into customer and donor data. This program was so successful, the organization has licensed the software to other Goodwill organizations and was awarded the SIM Innovation award in 2012.
- Catalyst for a multi-departmental team in the development and implementation of a student analysis system providing a first of its kind tool to educators throughout the state.
- Defined the strategy for the organization's approach to mission marketing including branding, messaging, market segmentation, and political advocacy.

BUILDITNOW, INC, Indianapolis, IN   2006 - 2008
Chief Information Officer and Vice President of Information Technology
Provided executive leadership as head of Enterprise Process, Information and Technology. Responsible for all aspects of IT strategic planning, implementation and support for this $600 million national commercial real estate development firm which experienced quadruple digit growth. Engineered turnaround of IT's performance and service levels and transformed IT into a strategic business partner. Full responsibility for P&L and multi-million dollar budget. Defined and implemented strategy for business processes, information and applications, infrastructure and technology.

- Created and implemented three year strategic plan covering process improvements, technology upgrades and network migration to support the business growth; achieving alignment with business leaders and company strategy.
- Led the re-engineering of the entire IT infrastructure of this complex commercial real estate development and construction business as it quadrupled in size reaching over $600 million in projects across 20 states.
- Implemented intra-company collaboration platforms allowing regional and satellite offices and job trailer personnel to work with headquarters associates more effectively.
- Led the transition of the IT department from the typical small business department to a true-value add business partner department for a mid-sized company in under two years, completing dozens of large scale projects on time and under budget.
- Built and managed a world class team of IT, process management, and business analyst professionals.
- Influenced all areas of the business through leadership of the BuildItNow Sustainability Initiative, Building Automation and Management, Great Service program, Servant Leadership program and BuildItNow Leadership Committee.

PRIOR EXPERIENCE

IT CONSULTANTS, INCORPORATED, Indianapolis, IN
1992-1998
TON HELLMANN AND ASSOCIATES, Indianapolis, IN
1989-1992

COMMUNITY COLLEGE (Instructor), Indianapolis, IN
1983-1984
ANY NATIONAL BANK, Indianapolis, IN
1979-1990

PROFESSIONAL ORGANIZATIONS & BOARDS

Indy CIO Network (Founder)
Institute for Digital Transformation (Institute Fellow)
Forbes Technology Council (Member)
Hoosier Environmental Council (Board member)
Mud Creek Conservancy (Board member)
Connected World Magazine (Board of Advisers)

EDUCATION & CERTIFICATIONS

MIT Executive Leadership Program, Cambridge, MA
LEED Accredited Professional (U.S. Green Building Council)
CCIM Candidate

78 AMPLIFY YOUR JOB SEARCH

reasonably sure you can solve his or her problem. The focus of the resume should be on what you can do for them, not on what you have done. You may not be a copywriter, but with a little bit of research and your Resume Amplifier, you can write a rock star resume!

Resume Amplifier

Martin Yate, author of the Knock 'Em Dead series of job search books, describes a great process for supercharging your resume. His process involves reviewing multiple job descriptions and extracting insights from them. We will be using the Resume Amplifier to guide that process. As you refine your job search, either by zeroing in on the title of the job you are seeking or by targeting a specific job title

RESUME AMPLIFIER WORKSHEET

TITLE	SKILLS	
	Skill	Rank (0-5)
Target Job Description		

Rank 0 = True Gap   5 = Rock Star

RESPONSIBILITIES		
Responsibility	Yrs.	Desire (1-5)

EXPERIENCES			DELIVERABLES		
Experience	Yrs.	# Acc.	Deliverable	Deliver	Sample
				Y/N	Y/N
				Y/N	Y/N
				Y/N	Y/N

(more on that in the section titled "Tailored Resume"), you will revisit the Resume Amplifier. You may even create separate ones for each job title you are interested in.

Job titles can be so confusing. Companies use different titles for the same job and the same title for dramatically different jobs. You may know how to describe the job you are seeking, but you may not know how that translates into a job title for your search. You may not know what you want to be when you grow up quite yet (even if you are sixty!). That's okay. Through your networking and research, you will get a better and better idea of the types of jobs that align with your Personal Brand Amplifier and your Accomplishment Amplifier. If you do know exactly what you want to be, that's great! You are ahead of the game.

If you have several types of jobs in mind, you will want to complete a Resume Amplifier on each one. Simply repeat the process for completing each one.

Search the internet for the type of job you have in mind. Don't limit yourself to a specific job title, location, or company. For this process, those things aren't important. These may or may not be positions for which you apply. For now, focus on the jobs in which you can excel and that align with your Personal Brand Amplifier and your Accomplishment Amplifier. Collect five or six examples.

In the Title section of your Resume Amplifier, write each one of the titles from your sample job descriptions. Congratulations! These are actual jobs for which you qualify and have interest in performing. Review the titles. Are there commonalities? Are the same words used in multiple titles? Is there a title that is most common? From these titles write a title of your own that encompasses the commonalities. This will be your target job description.

Say, for example, you are in human resources. You are seeking a leadership position in HR. You will find titles such as:

- Vice president human resources
- Director of human resources
- VP of people
- VP of human resources, Industrial Technique Services Division
- VP of employee success
- Chief people officer

You really like chief people officer. It describes your vision of what the job should be. However, of all the positions you find, the most common is vice president of human resources. Your target job description should be "vice president of human resources." You can tailor your target job description to match something more specific, like chief people officer when you tailor your resume to specific organizations and specific jobs.

Turn your attention to skills. Review each of your sample job descriptions. In the Skills section of your Resume Amplifier, list all the skills that appear in all of the sample jobs. Next, list all the skills that appear in all but one of the sample jobs, then the skills that are listed in all but two, all but three, and so on. Repeat until you are listing skills that only appear in one. You now know the skills employers need to solve the problems they are facing. Next to each skill, self-rank your competency in those skills on a scale of zero to five, zero being a true gap between the required skills and your skills, and five meaning you are a true rock star in that area.

Now, let's focus on responsibilities. In the Responsibilities section of your Resume Amplifier, list the responsibilities that appear in all the sample jobs. Repeat the process described above to complete this section. When you've completed listing the responsibilities, rank both your experience in holding that responsibility and your desire to hold that responsibility. Your experience should be in number of years. Your desire should be on a scale of one to five, one being "Ugh, that is not something I would like to do" and five being "Heck yeah, rock on!"

Repeat this process for the Experience section of the Resume Amplifier. After completing the list, rank your experience in both your years of experience and your accomplishments related to that experience. Accomplishments is the number of accomplishments listed in your Accomplishment Amplifier related to that experience or similar experience.

Finally, your sample job descriptions may list specific deliverables you would be required to produce in this role. To complete your Resume Amplifier, repeat the review process. When your list is complete identify the deliverables with a yes or no. Yes, you have created such a deliverable in the past, or no, you have not. For each yes answer, circle "Y" or "N" for each deliverable in your portfolio. Y for yes, you have a sample of that deliverable, or N for no, you do not.

In your Transition Journal, review the Resume Amplifier. Write down each of your target job titles. Answer the following questions:

1. I do or do not have the skill required to perform this job.
2. To excel at this job, I need to further develop my skills in [blank].

3. This job has responsibilities I love to do. They are: [blank]
4. This job has some responsibilities I don't care for. They are: [blank].
5. For the latter, I would do these things to mitigate or compensate: [blank]
6. My experience aligns well with the experience required. To tell that story, I will highlight these accomplishments: [blank]
7. My portfolio of deliverables is robust, but I do have some gaps. I will work to fill those gaps by: [blank]

As you write your resumes…Wait? What? Resumes? As in plural? How many resumes do I need?

Funny you should ask that…We'll get to that in a moment.

As you write your resumes, reference your Resume Amplifier for your target job title, skills, responsibilities, experience, and accomplishments. Use the terminology you found in the sample job descriptions.

A Bit about Style

Resume styles change. Do some research into resumes of others in similar professions. While you will want your resume to stand out from the stack, you don't want to differ too much from current styles.

Choose a typeface that is easy to read. Typefaces can evoke emotions in the reader. You want your reader to be comfortable, and you want them focused on the content of the resume, not on that new typeface. Stick with the basics and don't get carried away with using too many typefaces. Since you won't know if the reader is reading a printed page or reviewing it digitally, select a typeface that looks good on both. My recommendation is to use Arial.

As you write your resume, avoid playing cliché bingo. Avoid terms like *results-oriented*, *hands-on*, *people person*, and *self-starter*. (The exception to this rule is when the employer uses those words in their job descriptions. See the section titled "Tailored Resume" below.)

There is a lot of debate about the length of a resume. If your career spans more than five or ten years, there is no need to try to keep it to one page. It should be long enough to tell your story to the reader and no longer. You should try to keep it to two pages, or three at the most. You have a great story, but you're not writing a book!

Focus most of your attention on the top third of the first page of your resume. The reader's focus will be there. Their eyes will start there when they are scanning your resume. Make sure to lead with your strongest suit! This is where you want to set yourself apart from the competition.

Finally, proofread, proofread, and proofread some more. Nothing kills a great resume faster than typos, misspelled words, or poor grammar. Have two or three other people proofread it for you. Fix everything! Then proofread it again.

How Many Resumes Do I Need?

There are thousands of companies, each with its own process for hiring talent (people). Some use application tracking systems (ATS), some use third-party recruiters, some have in-house talent acquisition professionals, and some may have the hiring manager do all the screening. There are job boards, newspapers (yes, some still list jobs), industry newsletters, and social media sites that accept applications.

It is impossible for one resume, even if it is a killer resume, to work for every job, every company, or every channel.

You will need four types of resumes. Notice that I said *types* of resumes. These include LinkedIn (yes, LinkedIn is a resume; it may be the first resume someone sees), a bio resume, a general resume with a skills addendum, and a tailored resume (this is the general resume tailored to a specific job; you will have one for each position to which you apply).

For each type (excluding the LinkedIn resume type), you will have up to three formats for your resume: a word processing version (Word, Google Docs, etc.), a PDF version (to ensure the formatting remains intact), and a plain text version (to upload into some applicant tracking systems).

LinkedIn

LinkedIn has become the gold standard for a professional social media platform. To be successful in your search, you must have a presence on LinkedIn. In many cases, it will be the first place people go to learn about you. Remember, first impressions are important. You should spend as much time on your LinkedIn profile as you do on your resume itself—perhaps even more.

Your profile should be the online representation of your personal brand, with a focus on the professional. This means a high-quality headshot for the photo. Please, no selfies, no pictures with your spouse or kids or pets, and, unless you are applying for a job as a catcher for a baseball team, no backward baseball hats!

You should complete as many of the sections of the profile as you reasonably can, and each section should be as complete as possible. For example, the Experience section should contain the same work history as your printed resume. Each position should have a title, employment type, company, location, start and end dates, and a description. The description should describe your role and your accomplishments (just like on your resume). Don't take shortcuts. All this information should match your resume.

In addition to the headshot, the Intro section should contain a headline that is more than just a repeat of your recent title. It's a headline. Use it to sell your personal brand. Who *are* you? Here are some great examples:

- Business/IT Management | Transformational Leader | Authentic Innovator | Operations | IT Strategy
- Enabling gracious living, securely
- Breaking down the barriers between business and marketing
- Helping sales leaders unlock the full potential of their sales teams
- The #GratitudeDude, bringing purpose and gratitude to the workplace and generosity to the nonprofit space

You can also use a formula to build your headline. Remember, you have 120 characters, so each one needs to add value and grab attention. The formula is target job title | industry or expertise | your value. For example, "HR Executive | Putting people first in manufacturing | Diversity & inclusion champion."

Now, let's talk about the About section. If you are like me, this will be the hardest part to write. You are selling yourself, and sometimes selling ourselves is difficult. The prevailing school of thought is the About section should be written in the third person. Some feel that using "I" can come across as bragging. However, I have read some good ones that don't always follow that rule. Whether it's in third person or first person, the About section should sell who you are and what you can do.

This is another area you may want to consider using a professional copywriter. A copywriter is a professional writer who writes ad copy or promotional copy. Even though I am a professional author, I am not a skilled copywriter. I use a pro. Don't know a copywriter? I highly recommend Jennifer Brugh (https://www.linkedin.com/in/jrbrugh); she wrote mine. Of course, you can find dozens of outstanding copywriters on Thumbtack, TaskRabbit, and other gig style websites.

The About section should tell your story. Use your Personal Brand Amplifier. The About section should reflect your personal brand; it should tell people who you are and what you have done. Reference your Accomplishment Amplifier. Which accomplishments are you most proud of and why? Which ones speak to the story of your career? Include those (in highlight form) in your About section.

Here are some examples I really like, even though some of them may have broken some of the "rules."

Managing Executive

> If you wanted to change the world 400 years ago, you did it through religion; 200 years ago, you did it through government; today, you do it through business.

Jill's three passions are business, community service, and travel. Through early experiences, she discovered her purpose is to make the world a better place by connecting people via their differences. She plans to accomplish this as a social entrepreneur. So far, her journey includes: business - entrepreneur by age 10 and software executive by 23; community service - 7 years of non-profit work before founding a non-profit in 2018; travel - 17 countries and 6 continents. She is early on her journey to positively impact to world and energized about bringing others along for the adventure!

Top 5 Strength Finders: Activator, Strategic, Woo, Communication, and Competition.

XYZ Software is transforming workplace communications to transform the employee experience and make leaders better. As Managing Executive, Jill's job is to drive the firm's growth via strategy and sales leadership. She works closely with XYZ's customers and prospects to develop product strategies and communication tactics designed to help them effectively inspire employee engagement. She also leads XYZ's staff to expand their reach and drive positive customer experiences. By her work at XYZ, she is positively impacting leaders and emerging leaders, today, so they can positively impact their companies – and the world!

Digital Marketing Specialist

I am driven by the art of words, the conveying of ideas and the connecting of people. I am a masterful problem solver, calm under pressure and results driven. My endless curiosity results in constant learning; I've held licenses in real estate, esthetics and personal training. However, I've never been able to outrun the allure and craft of storytelling; repeatedly drawing me back to marketing. Even the numbers—especially the numbers—tell their own impartial tale.

- Marketing Strategy
- Branding
- Social Media & Digital
- Podcast Production
- Business Development
- Project Management
- Event Planning
- Sales Operations

Let's connect!

Project Manager

Accountable, Energetic, & Persistent

Innovative and energetic Servant Leader that drives effective communication among complex and diverse organizations of teams, projects, and initiatives with a knack for centering the development and implementation of effective solutions for multibillion-dollar enterprises. Highly skilled at project application and utilizing Agile frameworks to define and deliver program scope, policies, and milestones while partnering with stakeholders to align goals and project execution.

Talents & Strengths:

Program & Project Management Execution / Data Analysis & Documentation / Scrum & Agile Methodologies / 5S Strategic Planning / Operations Management / Relationship Cultivation & Maintenance / Continuous Improvements / Lean Six Sigma Application / Change Management / Communications & Presentations / Budgets & Deliverables / Root Cause Analysis / Scope of Work / P&L Management / Business Process Mapping / Risk Analysis / Quality Assurance / Leadership / Training / Customer Service

"The indispensable employee brings humanity and connection and art to [their] organization. [They are] the key player, the one who's difficult to live without, the person you can build something around…a person who's worth finding and keeping."
—Seth Godin

"The reward for work well done is the opportunity to do more."
—Jonas Salk

Vice President, Community College

> I am a wearer of many hats: I love solving problems using digital and communications solutions. I believe in technology not for the sake of technology, but because I've witnessed how technology influences change, resurrects and establishes brands, and positively impacts the bottom line. I am unafraid to follow process so I can influence it—or test its flexibility. I enjoy managing people; engaged employees are critical to the success for any organization.

I encourage you to read more on LinkedIn. Which ones stand out to you? Why? Read from inside and outside your network.

Bio Resume

Your bio resume is very similar to the About section of your LinkedIn profile. It tells people who you are in a few paragraphs and maybe a handful of bullet points. It is less detailed than a full resume. If you have ever spoken at a conference or been on a panel, this is your introduction. In fact, once you have bio resume, you can use it repeatedly for conferences.

For the purpose of landing your dream job, your bio resume is used to introduce yourself to networking contacts. As you have seen in chapters 4 and 5, networking is a significant part of your strategy. Very soon after embarking on your search, you will be meeting people whom you do not know and who don't know you. If you are meeting them for coffee face-to-face, bring a copy to share. The bio resume can also be sent prior to the meeting (I recommend you bring a hard copy to the meeting). If it is a virtual coffee meeting, of course, email the bio resume. As your network expands (and it will), have the person doing the introductions send it to the new contact to make a warm introduction even warmer. This also makes the task of making an introduction easier on the person doing the introduction.

Like the About section on LinkedIn, this should be written in the third person. If you are using a professional copywriter, tell them you would like two versions: one for LinkedIn and the other for networking. Have them include your headshot and some of the information from other sections of the LinkedIn profile (Job History, Accomplishments, Activities).

The website Grammarly has some great advice and some templates to use for writing your bio resume. When you are a job seeker, there are some key elements to include. Start with your name. Even if your name is on the page header, repeat it in the opening of your bio. Next up is your brand. For our purposes, this will be your personal brand. Refer to your Personal Brand Amplifier for some keywords to use. Add your current or most recent function or role. This will be the role most people know you by. Include a sentence or two about who you are: what makes you tick, your goals, your values. List your top three accomplishments. Review your Accompaniment Amplifier to find the three that really set you apart. Wrap up with a couple sentences about who you are when you are not working. This could include family, hobbies, and free time activities.

Remember to include your contact information, including your social media contacts.

General Resume

The general resume is your foundational resume. This will be the resume you submit to jobs when you know little to nothing about the position. Perhaps it is a listing in a newspaper or business journal. It gives very little insight into the requirements. The name of the company may even be obfuscated. In any case, you are unable to learn the specifics needed to tailor your resume to the position. This resume will also include a skills inventory addendum to further aid in winning against the algorithms of an applicant tracking system.

Application tracking systems are used at most companies today to help them handle the influx of applicants. These systems are used to store, sort, and report on the applications received. Many of these systems will score the application based on an algorithm before a human ever sees them. If you don't score above a certain threshold, you may receive an automated "Thanks, but no thanks" letter.

A rock star resume includes some specific sections.

Contact

Include your name, address, email address, phone number, social media links, portfolio link, and website link. Some people will opt not to include their address. I am a proponent of giving them every opportunity to contact you.

If you have a portfolio of work samples, such as presentations, speeches, blogs, or videos, include a link to it in the contact section. If you have created a website to promote your personal brand or career, be sure to include that link as well.

Take a moment to review your email address. Does it represent you in a way that supports your personal brand?

Cute email addresses are just that: cute. Is that what you want to convey as you network and interview for jobs? It's best to keep it simple and use your name combined with a meaningless number (not your birth year, graduation year, or some other date that reveals personal information). Set up a new email address today, if you need a new one.

Target Job Title

Add your target job title. This is the title of the job you want, not the title of the job you just had (unless, of course, that is the job you want). More on determining and tailoring your target job title later in this chapter.

Performance Profile

The performance profile can be as short as two or three sentences and as long as a paragraph or two (if it tells a compelling story). It could include your title (current or previous) or profession, years of experience, your top hard skills, and your top soft skills. However, it doesn't need to list them specifically. Remember, you are telling a story.

I recently interviewed Stephanie Gilbert, Talent Acquisition Manager at Givelify, about performance profiles. She stressed that the performance profile must go beyond recapping your experience. It must plant a picture in the recruiter's mind of your ability to meet the company's objectives today and your ability to grow and adapt in the future.

Stephanie provided some examples of resume performance profiles that stood out to her (and she reviews a *lot* of resumes).

Talent Acquisition Manager

Over 20 years of unique, progressive corporate promotions resulting in talent acquisition, Executive Search Recruiting and Management experience in all aspects of Human Resources:

• Created, established, managed, and maintained the following social media platforms for Acme & Roadrunner:

Twitter: @AcmeCareers #AcmeLife | Glassdoor | Indeed | LinkedIn | StackOverflow

Twitter: @RoadrunnerCareers #BecomeARoadrunner | Glassdoor | LinkedIn

• Training/Mentoring recruiters (entry level to senior level) • Work within the business and partner with hiring managers to obtain clear direction of open opportunities on their teams • Montréal, Québec, 2008: Hands-on Project Managed all sourcing, recruiting and interviewing of candidates for Interactive Intelligence's office location in Montréal, Québec • International recruiting and hiring throughout EMEA and APAC

Senior Accountant

Charita is a highly motivated accounting specialist with over seven years of experience assisting advisors in both the private and public practice industry. She has advanced experience building efficient financial reports, managing and planning tax duties for government entities, and forecasting future budgetary needs. Charita uses accounting software along with her presentation skills to supply local and national government offices with budget plans, which proves to reduce annual overall costs by 27%. In recognition of her public engagement and leadership, Charita has received several awards from a host of different organizations.

Full-Stack Engineer

In 2019, Juana earned a master's degree in computer science, but she soon learned her true passion was in UX design. Juana's programming background has helped her to automate most of her tasks along the way, and she eventually ended up in cloud computing, as it offered more possibilities. Juana is a full-stack engineer who has particularly strong development skills with all things AWS, to which her numerous certifications can attest. Her front-end development capabilities were strong enough to work an entire rebrand to a company, where she contributed significantly from end to end. Following this standout performance at XYZ Company, Juana flexed her teaching muscles for a while as a teaching fellow before acing ABC Company's application process, which landed her next career journey as a UX designer, working with this hot global giant!

Professional Skills/Qualifications

Include a table of your key professional skills or qualifications. These should be your top skills or qualifications. Review your list of skills for outdated, irrelevant, or ubiquitous skills. If you find any in your list, delete them!

You are trying to show the reviewer right away that you are qualified for this position. Later in this chapter we will discuss ways to build your list of skills and how to tailor this list to a specific job.

Work Experience

Refer to your PAR (problem, actions, results) analysis from chapter 3 and the resume bullets. Which ones tell your story? You will want to include those.

Include your work history for the last ten to fifteen years. If your career spans more than fifteen years, include prior positions only if they are relevant to your desired job. Consider listing older positions in summary form (years, company, title) only.

Work history should be listed in reverse chronological order, with the most recent appearing first.

For each position, include start and end dates, company, role or title, and a few lines describing your responsibilities. Using bullet points list your major accomplishments, again referencing your PAR analysis resume bullets. Include no more than six or seven bullets per role.

Use appropriate keywords in your description of your role and your accomplishments. There will be more information on keywords later in this chapter.

A word about gaps in your work history: If you have a gap in your career history of more than six months, explain it. The person reviewing your resume is going to wonder anyway. You might as well hit it head-on. Add a work experience entry for the gap. Include the same information you would if you were describing job experience, including accomplishments.

A word about frequent job changes: If you have had frequent job changes during the last ten to fifteen years, explain it. Again, the reviewer is wondering. Address it. Did a job change due to a merger or acquisition? Did the industry experience a downturn and therefore the company had a reduction in force? If you find it difficult to explain in the context of a resume, the reviewer is going to have a hard time understanding it. At the very least, be prepared to answer the question (asked or unasked) in an interview.

Education

List your education experience, including degrees earned. This section should also be in reverse chronological order. The entry should include the school, dates, degrees earned, and any honors received. GPA is irrelevant once you are a few years removed from your studies. Include any relevant continuing education you have completed since finishing your formal education.

Additional Experience

This section could also be labeled as "Candidate Facts," "Volunteerism," or "Hobbies." This is your opportunity to add color to your resume. Revisit the Passions section of your Personal Brand Amplifier. What experience can you write here that underscore those passions? Give the reviewer a sense of who you are and what makes you tick.

Don't be afraid to be quirky in this section. I once interviewed a person for a very technical role because they listed "Ability to rope a steer in under 9 seconds" on their resume. (I hired them, by the way.)

Skills Inventory Addendum

This is an addendum to your resume. Odds are your resume will find its way into an application tracking system. The reviewer will then pull resumes from the ATS through search criteria. Most ATSes today will also score your resume based on an algorithm that awards points based on keyword matching. When sending your general resume to apply for positions and you know very little about the position or the company, include your skills addendum.

On his website, ReCareered.com, career coach and recruiter Phil Rosenberg suggests that the skills inventory should list as many of your professional and technical skills you can fit on one page, single-spaced, in three columns. If you are in a technical field, such as information technology, three single-spaced columns should be the minimum you shoot for.

In the skills inventory you want to list some skills more than once, especially if the skill could be referenced in more than one way. For example, if you are in IT and are well versed in SD-WAN technology, list it as SD-WAN, SD WAN, software defined WAN, software defined wide area network, WAN, and wide area network. You have no way of knowing the keywords being used to select the resumes from the ATS, and you want your resume to be scored among the highest.

Remember, don't lie or stretch the truth, but if you have the skill, claim it!

There are two or three things not to include in your general resume. Unless you are specifically requested through a job posting to include a cover letter, don't. Cover letters tend to get read less than resumes (remember, resumes get six seconds), and the time spent reviewing your cover letter eats into the time your resume is being reviewed. Your resume should tell the story. If it does, your cover letter is redundant. If it doesn't…well, it should.

Next on the list of what not to include is an objective statement. Unless you are fresh out of college, you should use a performance profile instead. Objective statements tell the reader what you want. Of course you want a job. Of course you want the job they have available. Why else would your resume be on their desk? Remember, your resume is not about you. It is about the reviewer. Why should they interview you? What problem do they have that you are going to solve? How are you going to solve it? What's in it for them in the mind of the reviewer?

Finally, do not include references or even the statement "References available upon request." Of course, you must have references to back up your claims; you just don't need to list them on the resume. They only serve to take up space. The reviewer knows that when the time comes, you will provide references. They also know that their application system will require you to enter references, and that's where they will pull them from anyway.

Tailored Resume

Your tailored resume is just that: tailored. As you come across positions you are interested in, research each one. Hopefully, you will at least have a copy of the job description. If you are replying to an ad, it may be more difficult to obtain. Check out the company's website and job board. Gather as much information about the specific position and about the company.

Next, make a copy of your general resume. It will be easier for you to track if you add the company name and perhaps the position to the file name.

Review the copy and tailor it to the job description and the research you have uncovered.

- **Target Job Title:** This is the easiest one. Change your target job title to the one listed in the job description.
- **Keywords:** Scan the resume, looking for keywords and acronyms. Be sure you are using the same keywords or acronyms you found in your research. This is especially important in the skills areas of your resume. Use their words to describe your experience.
- **Emphasis:** In the Work Experience section, think about your points of emphasis. What is going to be more appealing to the reviewer, the company where you worked, the title(s) you held, or the

years? Highlight using bold type the element you think should stand out based on your research. Don't be afraid to name-drop; if you worked with key clients who are well known (and you are at liberty to disclose them), name them.
- **Specific Skills:** Where the job description or your research identifies specific skills, make sure your resume lists those skills (assuming, of course, you have those skills; resumes should not be a work of fiction).

Reflection

Time to pick up your Transition Journal. Review your Resume Amplifier. Where are the gaps? Reflect on ways you can close those gaps. How many job titles did you research? Which ones really stand out to you as you reflect on your Personal Brand Amplifier? Which ones stand out as you reflect on your Accomplishment Amplifier? Review your Network Amplifier. Who can help connect you to those jobs or those industries? Where are there gaps in your network?

Read back over your Transition Journal. What thoughts occur to you now? Is there anything you would change? Do you have any new insights into your journey?

7

Marketing–with a Twist

You now have a great foundation! You've developed your personal brand, identified your accomplishments, and started to build or expand your network, and you have a rockin' resume (four or more resumes, actually). It's been a lot of work, but you are well on your way to finding that dream job. Now what?

It may not come as a great surprise after reading the first several chapters that we are going to use a systematic, data-driven approach to your search.

You are now marketing and selling a product. That product is *you*! One of the first steps in marketing a product is determining your TAM, SAM, and SOM: your total available market, serviceable addressable market, and share of market. Not a marketer? Let's break it down.

TAM, SAM, and SOM decoded

The marketing and sales funnel will be familiar to many of you whether or not you are in marketing and sales. Even if you have the greatest product in the world, you

SALES FUNNEL

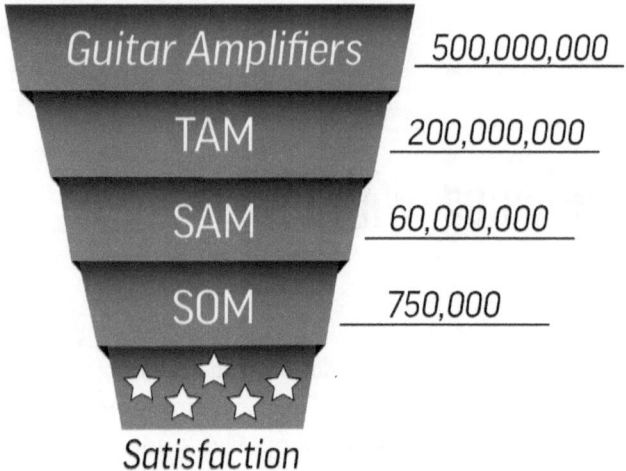

are not going to be able to sell it to everyone on the planet. The marketing and sales funnel describes the sales cycle from identifying possible customers to closing the sale. The TAM, SAM, and SOM represent the narrowing of the funnel as prospects are nurtured.

Total Available Market (TAM) is defined as the total market demand for a product or service. Let's say that instead of selling you, you were selling the next great guitar amplifier. You might do a quick search and learn there are 500 million guitar players worldwide. (That's a total guesstimate to be used for this example only. Do *not* attempt to build the next great guitar amplifier based on this example.) However, let's say only 40 percent of those guitar players are interested in electric guitars. That takes your market to 200 million.

Serviceable Addressable Market (SAM) is defined as the portion of the TAM targeted and serviced by a company's product or service. For our example, the majority of guitar players live in the United States or Europe. Your great new amplifier was designed in Nashville, Tennessee, and you intend to only target US guitarists. If 30 percent of the electric guitar players live in the US, your SAM is 60 million.

Share of Market (SOM) is defined as the portion of the SAM that can realistically be reached. Taking our amplifier story one step further, three companies control about 75 percent of the market. You determine that you can realistically reach 5 percent of the remaining 25 percent. So, 25 percent of 60 million guitar players is 15 million, and 5 percent of that number is 750,000. There are several other factors that would further reduce your SOM, such as the number of players expected to buy a new amp. But I think we have ridden this horse far enough.

SALES FUNNEL

YOU!
TAM ← All Jobs Everywhere
SAM ← Serviceable Jobs / SAM List
SOM ← Focused List
Your Dream Job

Okay, great. But I only need one job. What does all this have to do with my search? TAM equates to the shotgun approach, you know, the "any job will do" approach. How many employers are in the world? At the extreme, that is your TAM. Even if you add a dose of reality and limit it to the number of employers that employ people in your profession, it is still a big number. Too big of a number to find your dream job, like finding a needle in a haystack.

How do we begin to narrow down the funnel? We take a cue from David Letterman (yes, that David Letterman).

Amplify Your Job Search's Top Ten Lists

The next tool in our tool belt is the SOM Amplifier. Its job is to help you narrow down the hundreds of thousand businesses and jobs to a much more manageable list. The first section of the SOM Amplifier is Amplify Your Job Search's Top Ten Lists. Like Letterman's but much less funny (unless, of course you are vying for the job of late-night TV host).

On a piece of paper, make a list of the top ten things you are looking for in your next position. Use your Personal Brand Amplifier, Accomplishment Amplifier, Network Amplifier, and Resume Amplifier to aid you in compiling the list. It's okay if you list more than ten.

Finished with the list? Good. Now force rank them 1 to 10, no ties, where 1 is the most important thing you are looking for in your next job, and 10 is the least important of your top ten. Write the ranked list in the Next Position section of your SOM Amplifier.

Next, repeat the process by creating a list of the top ten things you are looking for in your next boss and then the top ten things you are looking for in your next company.

SOM AMPLIFIER WORKSHEET
AMPLIFY YOUR JOB SEARCH • TOP TEN LISTS

NEXT POSITION		NEXT BOSS		NEXT COMPANY	
	SCORE		SCORE		SCORE
☐		☐		☐	
☐		☐		☐	
☐		☐		☐	
☐		☐		☐	
☐		☐		☐	
☐		☐		☐	
☐		☐		☐	
☐		☐		☐	
☐		☐		☐	
☐		☐		☐	

Each Top 10 List scores a max of 55 points.

SEARCH CRITERIA		
FIELD	OPERATOR	VALUE

Force rank each of those lists and then copy them to the corresponding section of your SOM Amplifier.

This exercise will force you to think about the traits in your next job that would make it your dream job. We will use these lists in two ways. First, they will become your search criteria, and later you will use them to evaluate multiple offers to select the one that meets most of your criteria.

Before moving on to the next step, go back to your Resume Amplifier. How many of the skills and responsibilities listed there show up on your SOM Amplifier? If there are significant differences, consider repeating the Resume Amplifier exercise and using your Next Position

Top Ten List as your search criteria as you search for job descriptions.

Time to Go to the Library

Actually, you may not even need to go to the library, but you will probably need a library card.

Several years ago, I founded a company. Our TAM were small businesses who were in the professional services sector, businesses such as law firms, accounting practices, insurance brokers, and financial advisors. We needed to grow. We didn't know how. I was told about the free services from the Small Business Administration. Wow! Free? Can't beat that price. I signed up and went to meet with an advisor. He gave me *tons* of advice. The piece of advice that proved to be the most valuable then and in every job search since was to use the library's free database of registered companies to search for companies that matched my target market. Get where we are going here?

Call your public library. No, I mean now. Go call them. I'll wait. Find out if they provide access to Mergent Intellect. Mergent Intellect is a database of over 265 million business records from around the world. If your public library does not provide access, check with the university libraries in your area. Finally, if you can't get access, contact Mergent to ask them how to get access in your area.

Log in to the database and go to "Search," then "Advanced Search." Familiarize yourself with the search criteria available. On your Next Company Top Ten List, flag the items in your list that are searchable within Mergent. Identify other search criteria that would be useful. Run some searches as practice. The goal is to use as many criteria from your Next Company Top Ten List in your searches as you can. Write the search criteria on your SOM Amplifier.

I spent most of my career in information technology. At one point I was seeking a position of chief information officer (CIO). My Next Company Top Ten List included:

- **Location:** Central Indiana (I did not want to relocate). I defined Central Indiana as the seventeen counties surrounding Indianapolis.
- **Size:** More than 250 employees (any fewer than that and they would not need a strategic thinking CIO) and less than 3,000 employees (I'd worked for a large corporation, got the T-shirt, didn't need another).
- **Socially or environmentally conscious or both:** More on these later.

There were others, but these will suffice for our example.

Turning to Mergent, I knew there was not a way to search on the criteria of a company's consciousness, but I could search on location and size. I also discovered a flag within the advanced search that allowed me to limit the search results to only companies headquartered within the location criteria. My rationale was the CIO would typically work at the headquarters.

My search results returned over 2,000 companies. Quite a nice addressable market when I only needed to find one that was looking for a strategic-thinking CIO. I'd never heard of most of those 2,000—yet. But I probably drove by many of them every day and had not "seen" them.

When you are happy with your search criteria, export the results to a CSV file to allow you to manipulate it in a spreadsheet. One of the drawbacks I faced was an export limit of twenty records. So yes, I ran and exported 100 lists and then combined them into my spreadsheet of 2,000 rows. Mergent no longer has this limitation. You now have a realistic TAM.

From TAM to SAM

A list of 2,000 companies is great, but hardly manageable. Your next task is to reduce the list to a more manageable number. Use the remainder of your Next Company Top Ten List to eliminate some of the companies (at least for now).

Remember my criteria of a socially or environmentally conscious company? I couldn't really search on that, although today I could probably identify companies with a corporate sustainability program. At the time, I looked at the line of business (LOB) and the standard industrial classification (SIC) codes in my search results and made some arbitrary decisions based on those. It was an inexact science, to be sure. I also eliminated duplicates, companies whose reputation led me to drop them, and anyone in construction or real estate development. No offense to those industries, but I had just lived through the crash of 2008 and 2009; I did not want to get back into that space.

Through these assumptions, some company research, and reducing the number of miles I wanted to drive I was able to get the list down to about 200. That became my SAM. Now, I just needed to find my SOM! My SAM List looked something like the figure.

As you review the data Mergent provides on the companies in your list, you will find a lot of very useful information, such as key staff, annual sales, year founded, and more. You may have noticed while exploring the search

SAM LIST EXAMPLE

Company Name	Ticker	Location	Location Type	Sales	SIC	URL	Phone Number
SIMON PROPERTY GROUP, INC	SPG	INDIANA(USA)	Headquarters	$5,795,189,000	67080000	WWW.SIMON.COM	(317) 636-1600
AMERICAN UNITED MUTUAL INSURANCE HOLDING COMPANY		INDIANA(USA)	Headquarters	$4,158,386,598	62110902	WWW.ONEAMERICA.COM	(317) 285-1877
COMMUNITY HEALTH NETWORK, INC		INDIANA(USA)	Headquarters	$2,076,911,000	80620000	WWW.CHNINC.COM	(317) 355-1411
REPUBLIC AIRWAYS HOLDINGS INC	RJETQ	INDIANA(USA)	Headquarters	$1,344,000,000	45120902	WWW.YOURRAHWORKPLACE.COM	(317) 484-6000
NATIONAL COLLEGIATE ATHLETIC ASSOCIATION		INDIANA(USA)	Headquarters	$1,118,496,545	86990100	WWW.NCAA.ORG	(317) 917-6222
CITIZENS ENERGY GROUP		INDIANA(USA)	Headquarters	$711,450,000	49240000	WWW.CITIZENENERGYGROUP.COM	(317) 924-3341
WILHELM CONSTRUCTION, INC		INDIANA(USA)	Headquarters	$665,000,000	15420101	WWW.FAWILHELM.COM	(317) 359-5411
NATIONAL WINE & SPIRITS, INC		INDIANA(USA)	Headquarters	$287,905,405	51820100	WWW.NWSCORP.COM	(317) 636-0292
ASPHALT MATERIALS, INC		INDIANA(USA)	Headquarters	$240,710,097	29510201	WWW.ASPHALT-MATERIALS.COM	(317) 872-6010
THE HEALTH & HOSPITAL CORP OF MARION COUNTY		INDIANA(USA)	Headquarters	$214,193,000	80620000	WWW.HHCORP.ORG	(317) 221-2000
HERITAGE ENVIRONMENTAL SERVICES INC		INDIANA(USA)	Headquarters	$206,409,565	50930909	WWW.HERITAGE-ENVIRO.COM	(317) 243-0811
MONARCH BEVERAGE CO., INC		INDIANA(USA)	Headquarters	$204,632,217	51819902	WWW.MONARCH-BEVERAGE.COM	(317) 612-1313
ADVANTAGE HEALTH SOLUTIONS, INC.		INDIANA(USA)	Single Location	$186,703,725	63249903		(317) 573-2700
FAEGRE BAKER DANIELS LLP		INDIANA(USA)	Single Location	$170,235,297	81119902	WWW.FAEGREBD.COM	(317) 237-0300
IVY TECH FOUNDATION, INC		INDIANA(USA)	Headquarters	$166,090,169	62229901	WWW.IVYTECH.EDU	(317) 921-4882
INDIANAPOLIS AIRPORT AUTHORITY		INDIANA(USA)	Headquarters	$160,672,462	45810301	WWW.INDIANAPOLISAIRPORT.COM	(317) 487-9594
MATERIALS PROCESSING, INC.		INDIANA(USA)	Headquarters	$159,252,927	50510000	WWW.MPICORP.COM	(317) 803-3010
TECHKNISA, LLC		INDIANA(USA)	Headquarters	$156,834,171	50840000	WWW.TECHNIKSUSA.COM	(317) 803-8000
BARNES & THORNBURG LLP		INDIANA(USA)	Headquarters	$151,022,265	81119902	WWW.BTLAW.COM	(317) 236-1313
UNIVERSITY OF INDIANAPOLIS		INDIANA(USA)	Headquarters	$122,248,263	82210102	WWW.UINDY.EDU	(317) 788-3368
ABC EMPLOYMENT HOLDINGS, LLC		INDIANA(USA)	Single Location	$120,369,077	73610101	WWW.MSCOMPANIES.COM	(866) 974-7679
TUBE PROCESSING CORP		INDIANA(USA)	Headquarters	$118,968,993	33560001	WWW.TUBEPROC.COM	(317) 787-1321
ERMCO, INC		INDIANA(USA)	Single Location	$114,988,504	17319903	WWW.ERMCO.COM	(317) 780-2923
MARIAN UNIVERSITY, INC		INDIANA(USA)	Headquarters	$107,232,933	82210101	WWW.MARIAN.EDU	(317) 955-6000
ICE MILLER LLP		INDIANA(USA)	Headquarters	$94,574,989	81119901	WWW.ICEMILLER.COM	(317) 236-2100
GOODWILL OF CENTRAL AND SOUTHERN INDIANA, INC		INDIANA(USA)	Headquarters	$92,797,237	56419901	WWW.GOODWILLINDY.ORG	(317) 664-4313
FIRE CHIEFS OFFICE		INDIANA(USA)	Single Location	$79,800,000	35890200		
INDIANAPOLIS PUBLIC TRANSPORTATION CORPORATION		INDIANA(USA)	Single Location	$70,115,055	41110101	WWW.INDYGO.NET	(317) 614-9221
CHILDREN'S MUSEUM OF INDIANAPOLIS INC		INDIANA(USA)	Headquarters	$62,463,447	84129902	WWW.CHILDRENSMUSEUM.ORG	(317) 924-5431
INDIANA VERITI INC		INDIANA(USA)	Headquarters	$61,374,471	80710103	WWW.INDIANABLOOD.ORG	(317) 916-5150
MAJOR TOOL AND MACHINE INC		INDIANA(USA)	Headquarters	$49,273,179	75920000	WWW.MAJORTOOL.COM	(317) 636-6433
72 UES, INC		INDIANA(USA)	Headquarters	$48,000,000	87119903	WWW.72UE.COM	(965) 222-8263
ADULT AND CHILD MENTAL HEALTH CENTER INC		INDIANA(USA)	Single Location	$47,893,305	80539902	WWW.ADULTANDCHILD.ORG	(317) 381-5200
POINDEXTER EXCAVATING INC		INDIANA(USA)	Single Location	$41,467,569	17040501	WWW.POINDEXTEREXCAVATING.COM	(317) 823-0837
AMERICAN INSTITUTE OF TOXICOLOGY, INC		INDIANA(USA)	Single Location	$40,713,414	87310103	WWW.AIIIFORTOX.COM	(317) 243-3894
BARTH ELECTRIC CO INC		INDIANA(USA)	Single Location	$39,000,000	17319903	WWW.BARTHELECTRIC.COM	(317) 924-6226
DEWALT CONSTRUCTION PARTNERS		INDIANA(USA)	Single Location	$38,800,000	15210000		(317) 979-6169
MS COMPANIES, LLC		INDIANA(USA)	Single Location	$38,451,006	73890200	WWW.MSCOMPANIES.COM	(317) 332-9311
CONBONA ERP INC		INDIANA(USA)	Single Location	$35,800,000	73710100	WWW.MADE2MANAGE.CONBONA.COM	(317) 249-1200
ASSURANCE HEALTH SYSTEM LLC		INDIANA(USA)	Headquarters	$34,620,993	80620000	WWW.ASSURANCEHEALTHSYSTEM.COM	(317) 870-1396
CONVENTION HEADQUARTERS HOTELS, LLC		INDIANA(USA)	Headquarters	$34,414,630	70110303	WWW.JWINDY.COM	(317) 860-5600
CAPITAL IMPROVEMENT BOARD OF MANAGERS		INDIANA(USA)	Single Location	$34,296,220	65120000	WWW.IGCLOB.COM	(317) 262-3400
SCHNEIDER ENGINEERING CORP		INDIANA(USA)	Headquarters	$32,853,705	87130000	WWW.SCHNEIDERCORP.COM	(317) 826-7100
MS INSPECTION & LOGISTICS, LLC		INDIANA(USA)	Single Location	$32,576,352	73890200	WWW.MS-IL.COM	(317) 322-9311
BOSE MCKINNEY & EVANS LLP		INDIANA(USA)	Headquarters	$31,825,776	81119902	WWW.BOSELAW.COM	(317) 684-5000

Source: Mergent Intellect. June 2020.

criteria that the information returned also includes job postings! This is a new way to search for job descriptions and potential jobs.

Other Sources

As you build your SAM List, use other sources to add to your list. Most metropolitan areas have a local business journal. Many of them produce lists of companies and keep them updated. Reviewing these could provide companies to include.

As you network, you will be talking with dozens of people about their careers. Ask about the companies where they worked. If they loved them (and they fit your SOM Amplifier criteria), include them. If they didn't care for them, consider taking them off your list, depending on the reasons. I dropped a company from my list when I learned that their CEO stood vocally on the other side of an issue I care deeply about.

Reflection

Time to pick up your Transition Journal. Review your SOM Amplifier and your SAM List. Are you satisfied with the search results? Pick several companies from your spreadsheet. Can you imagine yourself working for those organizations? Spend some time thinking about that future. Picture yourself commuting to their location, parking, walking in. What do you feel?

Read back over your Transition Journal. What thoughts occur to you now? Anything you would change? Any new insights into your journey?

8
Ready? Set? Go!

You now have all the tools you need to find a job. Not just a job...*the* job. You've spent time developing your personal brand with your Personal Brand Amplifier. You've recalled all your past accomplishments using your Accomplishment Amplifier. You have started to build an amazing and diverse network with your Network Amplifier. You've written, not one, not two, not three, but four killer resumes leveraging your Resume Amplifier. Finally, you have built your serviceable addressable market (SAM) list using your SOM Amplifier.

Now is the time to put them all together. Now is the time to get social.

Time Is on Your Side

At the outset of this book, I told you that 87 percent of jobs are filled through professional networks. That does not mean that job boards, company websites, industry newsletters, and, yes, the newspaper are to be ignored in your search. They are all important tactics to support your job search strategy.

I also said that when you are in transition, your job is to find a job. That means full days dedicated to your search. If you are currently employed and want to find *the* job, you will still have to dedicate some serious time to your search. That can be a challenge, but in either case, the key is spending your most valuable resource—your time—on the most valuable activities.

What are the most valuable activities? The activities that help you land your dream job: networking activities! Let's assume you have eight hours a day to devote to your search. If 87 percent of jobs are filled through networking, you are going to want to spend 87 percent of your time on building, maintaining, and working your network! That's seven out of eight hours! That is a *lot* of coffee!

That leaves an hour a day for other activities like reviewing job boards, company websites, industry newsletters, and the newspaper. Of course, these tools can and do play a role in your networking strategy, as you will see.

Keeping Track of It All

As you search for a job, you may be talking to hundreds of people from dozens of companies and applying for a multitude of positions. How do you keep track of it all? LinkedIn used to provide some nice functionality to help you keep track of some of the information you are going to need as you network, but they moved that into their Sales Navigator tool. You could use Sales Navigator, but it will cost you several hundred dollars a year.

If you have ever worked in sales, you know the answer already: a customer relationship management application, or CRM! It's the sales pro's most valuable tool other than their phone. A CRM helps sales professionals keep track of hundreds of contacts and dozens of companies. Sound like a familiar problem? It also helps them keep track of potential sales or deals. Remember, throughout this book, I have stated that you are now in sales. You are selling a product, and that product is you. So? If you are selling you, then what is a potential sale or deal? An application submitted for a job, of course.

There you have it. You can use a CRM to track your connections (contacts), your target employers (companies), and your applications (deals or opportunities). But wait? Don't CRM applications cost hundreds, if not thousands of dollars? Well, some do. Some don't. HubSpot has a great CRM application and it is absolutely free! Visit HubSpot.com and get started today. They even have a great tutorial to get you started. If you use Gmail, HubSpot can be integrated so every email you send to one of your network connections is tracked. Pretty sweet!

Just keep in mind that where HubSpot says "Deal," you think "Application." To help you remember, there is small customization you should do. Don't worry—it's easy. Go to the Deals tab (it's under the Sales menu). HubSpot will display a list of all your deals. It's probably empty, but that's okay. It won't be for long. Near the top right is a selection that says "Edit Stages." Click that and HubSpot will take you the settings for deals. Part of the way down the page, you will see the default stage names. You can change them to whatever makes sense, but I recommend changing the following:

- "Appointment Scheduled" to "Application Submitted"
- "Qualified to Buy" to "Interview Scheduled"

- "Presentation Scheduled" to "Interview Completed"
- "Decision Maker Bought-In" to "Second Interview Scheduled"
- "Contract Sent" to "Second Interview Completed"
- "Closed Won" to "Job Offer Accepted"
- "Closed Lost" to "Job Lost"

You could add additional stages, perhaps "Third Interview," "Offer Received" or "Negotiation." I suggest you start simple; you can always add stages later.

SOM Amplifier Revisited

Let's refer to your SOM Amplifier and your SAM List, your target market. Somewhere in that list is your dream job, working for a great boss, at an outstanding company. The question is, how do you find it? Through networking, of course! (Come on, I set you up for that softball!)

When you aren't already having coffee with someone in your network, you are going to use your SOM Amplifier to create new networking opportunities. Let's see how it's done.

What's the first company on your SAM List? Go to LinkedIn. Do a company search for that company. Select the company from the search list.

Before going any further, take some time and look around. If you are not familiar with the company page on LinkedIn, explore the information available. You can learn a lot about an organization without even visiting their website.

- **Home:** Brief description, recent posts, recent posted jobs, affiliated pages, similar pages

- **About:** A more in-depth description, website, industry, size, headquarters, type, year founded and specialties
- **Jobs:** Another source of great information on posted jobs
- **People:** High-level analytics on the employees of the company who are on LinkedIn and a directory of everyone at the company on LinkedIn
- **Videos:** Videos the company has posted on LinkedIn
- **Ads:** Ads the company has posted on LinkedIn

On the right side of the Company header on the home page are two pieces of information that enable you to search connections. It will say, for example, "See all 363 employees on LinkedIn."

Above that, if you have any connections at that company, it will say, for example, "Jill Smith & 27 other connections work here."

Let's click on the "Jill Smith & 27 other connections work here." Twenty-eight people in your network work for one of the companies on your SAM List. It is possible this is your SOM (uh, share of market…You know, the company that is going to hire you). That's twenty-eight people you can talk to about what it is like to work there. Twenty-eight people who can help you find out how many of your Amplify Your Job Search's Top Ten List items you can check off. Twenty-eight people who can serve as a reference.

Okay, perhaps we are getting a bit ahead of ourselves. You don't even know if your dream job is open. Remember the Jobs page? Might as well click on that. Is your dream job listed? No? You didn't think it was going to be *that* easy, did you?

If you are lucky enough that the first company on your SAM List has your dream job open *and* you are connected to twenty-eight different people at the company. Start networking…right after you run out and buy a Powerball ticket! Seriously, skip to "Good Connections" in this chapter and get networking!

Let's say you aren't quite that lucky. You do have twenty-eight connections at your dream company. Do any of them already have your dream job? Start there. Reach out. Remember, the purpose of your networking is to find your dream job. The purpose of each networking meeting is to learn.

No one in your connections at this company has your dream job? Check the rest of the employees on LinkedIn. Does anyone have that job? If so, are they connected to any of your twenty-eight connections? They're connected to Jill? Excellent. Reach out to Jill and invite her to coffee. "Hi, Jill. I hope this note finds you well. As you know, I am in transition from my job at Acme Corporation. Roadrunner is a company I am interested in learning more about. Let's do coffee. I would love to talk to you about the company and your role there."

While at coffee, say, "Jill, thank you for sharing your story and your experience at Roadrunner. It sounds like a great place to be. I know Bob Smith is your director of product management. As you know, product management is my dream job. Would you be willing to introduce me to Bob? I would love to talk to him about his story and learn more about his role at Roadrunner."

You may be asking why you would want to spend time talking with Jill and Bob, if Bob already has your job. You never know. Bob may be thinking of leaving. Bob may be in the process of getting promoted. Bob may know of three other companies like Roadrunner who need great directors of product management. You are pulling on threads to see what unravels.

Of course, if in your review of the employees at Roadrunner, you don't see anyone there with your dream job, you still want to have coffee with Jill and some of her twenty-seven coworkers. You are now playing detective to uncover the mystery of who has that job...if anyone.

Take the time now to enter the company into your CRM or tracking tool (it's okay to use spreadsheets; it just gets a little more cumbersome to track). If you are using HubSpot, you will only need the domain name (or URL for their website) and the name of the company. It will fill in additional information. Compare that information to your SAM List and make note of the differences.

You won't need to enter all twenty-eight connections into the CRM or your tracking tool, however, as you reach out to make connections at the company, add those as contacts in your CRM.

Hmmm...What's This Thread?

Several years ago, when I was in transition, I built my SOM Amplifier and my SAM List. As I mentioned in a previous chapter, it had about 200 companies listed. At the time, I was looking for a chief information officer role. One of the first companies listed in my SOM was Columbus Regional Health, a hospital in Columbus, Indiana. It fit several of my Next Company Top Ten List items.

I went to LinkedIn and did a company search. I did not have any first- or second-degree connections with anyone there. As I reviewed the employees from Columbus

Regional, I found the CIO listed. I admit to being a little disappointed that my dream job was filled, but not to be deterred, I reached out to her and wrote: "I am a CIO in transition. I am expanding my network and would love to connect."

Very simple and to the point. A few days later she accepted my connection. To which I responded: "Thank you very much for accepting my connection request. As I mentioned, I am a CIO in transition. Would you be willing to jump on a call? I would love to learn more about a day in the life of a CIO at a hospital."

To my delight, she agreed, and we scheduled a thirty-minute call.

Now, it would be a great story if I told you when we talked, she confessed that she was leaving the hospital and was so impressed with me in one thirty-minute call that she offered me the job to be her replacement. It would be a great story…but not a true one.

What did transpire was a great and very helpful conversation. After learning a lot about the challenges of running IT for a hospital and her career story, I shared mine briefly. She said, "You know, Jeff. No hospital is going to hire you to be CIO. You don't have healthcare experience. They are not going to want to take the time to train you. They won't want that risk."

Air out of my sails. But she continued:

> But here are a couple of thoughts. What about electronic records management software companies? There are a couple in Indianapolis. I know they are hiring because they keep poaching my people. You could work for them for a couple years and get healthcare

experience, learn the lingo, and then perhaps make the jump to a hospital.

Or, have you considered senior living owners and operators? They have the same records management requirements we do, and most of them are a few years behind. They may be more apt to take a chance on someone with your background, especially given your experience in commercial real estate development.

Two amazing suggestions. I checked my SAM List. There was a senior living organization listed. I moved them up in priority. I also quickly researched for others in the area and added them to the SAM. New leads! While I was at it, I researched electronic records management software companies and did indeed find three in my area. I added those to my list.

That is how this works. By having conversations with people and listening to their stories, you learn more about them and their work, and you gain valuable insights and new threads to pull on.

Preparation: The Difference between Winning and Losing

Any athlete will tell you that preparation is the difference between winning and losing. This is also true for being successful in finding your dream job. Preparation is vital. In addition to using LinkedIn to learn about the companies on your SAM List, there are dozens and dozens of other resources available to you: company websites, Glassdoor, Google (go beyond page 1), and social media.

Remember, you are trying to learn all you can about the company. After all, they may be your dream company.

Follow them on social media platforms like LinkedIn, Facebook, Twitter, Instagram, and other places you can find them. What are they posting? What are people saying about them? What jobs do they have open? Consider using an aggregator tool to centralize all the information. I use Hootsuite. It enables me to set up streams to sort the vast amount of information into useful categories: by company, by industry, by keywords.

Not only should you research the companies on your SAM List, but you should perform the same level of research on anyone you are meeting as part of your networking activities. Use LinkedIn, Google, and social media. Use the information to get to know them. What are they posting? What are they liking? Use the information to jot down a few questions to ask them when you meet.

Connections

As you begin to target your networking at specific companies from your SAM List, you will want to get more intentional about with whom you are networking. You are probably not going to invite all twenty-eight people you are connected to at Roadrunner to coffee.

- How well do you know them?
- How likely are they to give you candid feedback on the company?
- How long have they been at the company?
- How many people are they connected with at the company?
- Where are they in the organization's hierarchy?

Of course, if you know of a specific opening or role at the company that could be your dream job, these questions deserve even more scrutiny. You will need a connection who has influence within the company. Some of the questions above can be an indication of influence. Identify your best connections and invite them to coffee. Your invitation should also be clear that you are interested in the opening, but you still want to approach networking as a listening exercise. You want to know their story. After all, you are evaluating their company as much as they soon will be evaluating you.

The Ask

You may recall from the chapter on networking that your networking meetings are going to end with two asks. Your first and most important ask is "What can I do for you?" If they defer and say they can't think of anything, your research prior to the meeting may have given you some ideas of how you can help them. Are there articles you can share? Any books you can recommend? Can you make any introductions?

Your second ask is "Who else should I be meeting?" Your goal should be to walk away with the names of three people your contact has committed to making a warm introduction to on your behalf. You may need to be specific and ask for the warm introduction.

Just as your networking becomes more targeted when there is a specific opening you are interested in, your ask becomes more targeted. "Who else at Roadrunner could provide additional insights into the opening for the controller? Would you be willing to introduce me to them? I would like to learn more." Or "Do you know the hiring manager for the controller position? I would love to talk to them about their needs beyond what I have learned from the job description. Would you be willing to introduce me?"

If they are not comfortable introducing you to the hiring manager, you could suggest they reach out to the hiring manager and inquire if they would be open to the introduction. That may be an easier ask of them.

What you are trying to avoid are answers like "Go ahead and apply to the position and I will put in a good word with HR" or "Send me an electronic copy of your resume and I will pass it along to HR."

While those can be helpful, your first choice is a warm introduction to the hiring manager. If they are not comfortable with an introduction, ask them to forward your resume to the hiring manager with a sentence or two about your conversation and their impression of you as a viable candidate.

No Connection

What if you were not connected to Jill or her twenty-seven coworkers? Review the employees who are on LinkedIn. Do you have any second-degree connections with any of them? Are there one or two with whom you have multiple shared connections? Reach out to those shared connections. Ask them for an introduction. Most people will be open to making an introduction.

Don't even have a second-degree connection? In my experience, trying to get a third-degree connection to introduce you to a second-degree connection to gain an introduction rarely is successful. You are better off reaching out to individuals in the company seeking a connection. Use the feature in LinkedIn that allows you to customize the connection request message. Tell them you are in transition and are interested in learning about the company. Would they be open to a connection and possibly a phone call? It *does* work!

There Is an Opening...Go for It!

As you work your way through your SAM List, follow up on threads, review job boards, and network, you will identify positions that have the potential to be your dream job. There are several schools of thought about when to apply to the position via the company's website.

Do your research. Try to find out as much as you can about the job. Use some of the tactics described in this chapter to learn about the company, your connections, and the role. While you want to learn as much as you can, you also don't want to take so much time that the company closes the posting or gives your dream job to someone else.

Once you have done enough research to determine it has the potential to be your dream job, create your tailored resume for the position. Now you can apply for the position. Many companies will ask that you upload your resume. Be sure you have either a PDF copy or a plain text copy of your tailored resume.

Update your CRM or tracking tool with the job title and the date you submitted your application. As you network, your connections will want to know the specific title you are interested in. It will help them make the appropriate introductions.

Continue networking with this company and the others on your SAM List.

Reflection

By now, writing in your Transition Journal should be second nature. Carve out time every day to track your thoughts in your journal. (Of course, you are going to track this in your CRM or tracking tool as well.) Whom have you talked with? What did you learn? Does it refine your approach? What new threads did you pull on?

Do you have any adjustments to make to your Personal Brand Amplifier? Your Accomplishment Amplifier? Your Network Amplifier? Your Resume Amplifier? Your SOM Amplifier? Update those tools, and reflect in your journal about what helped you realize you needed to make the changes.

9
Let's Get Creative

What a journey we have been on together! We defined your personal brand with your Personal Brand Amplifier. We looked back on a career of accomplishments as we built your Accomplishment Amplifier. We've supercharged your networking by using your Network Amplifier. You now have a rockin' resume through your Resume Amplifier. We've zeroed in on your target market for your laser approach to finding your dream job with the SOM Amplifier and SAM List. Finally, we have leveraged your network through LinkedIn, Twitter, Facebook, and other platforms to launch your search.

What's that you say? You still aren't getting interviews? Now might be the time to get creative!

Kickin' It up a Notch

Remember the story from chapter 6? The "I can rope a steer in 9 seconds" story? That one line, that one risk got that person the interview. He took a chance. Honestly, I do not know how much he fretted over putting that on his resume. I do know that one line got his resume reviewed far longer than the average six seconds. I also know that he got not only the interview but the job. Oh, and by the way, if you ever met him, the last thing you would think was "cowboy." However, he really did learn how to rope a steer at a "cowboy camp" he vacationed at one year (remember the movie *City Slickers*?).

Sometimes it pays to get creative in your job search. How creative you get may depend on your comfort with taking the risk. It may also depend on the industry or the role you are seeking. Writing a little ditty and performing a music video might grab the attention of an ad agency looking for creative talent, but it probably won't be effective for a medical director at a hospital.

The Rest of the Story...

Speaking of hospitals, remember the story I told you in the last chapter? The story of reaching out to the CIO of a local hospital and the suggestions she gave me for follow-up? Let me finish that story. As you recall, she suggested I consider looking into senior living facilities and their technology leader needs as a potential next step in my career. I took her up on her advice. Through my research, I added several organizations to my SAM List.

But I went beyond just adding the company names to my list. I researched the industry with a focus of gaining an understanding of the technology needs for senior living organizations at that time and several years into the future. I began to get some idea of what types of things I might do as a CIO for such an organization.

As I looked at the senior living companies in my SAM List, I focused on one. It seemed to be one of the largest. It seemed to check off several of the items on my Next Company Top Ten List. Here was the problem. I had no connections—zero, zip, zilch. Not only that, but I couldn't find anyone associated with technology at their company on LinkedIn. After failing to make any headway after several conversations within my network, I thought I would get creative. I sat down and wrote a letter to the CEO. (By the way, unless you are seeking an executive-level position, I don't recommend blindly contacting the CEO.)

Oh, and I mean a letter. An actual letter: stationery, envelope, stamp, US Postal Service. In that letter I described some of the challenges within the industry I had read about in my research. This ranged from the obvious, like electronic records management, to the not so obvious, like aging baby boomers who are becoming more connected and the demands they would place on internal Wi-Fi networks.

I went on to admit that I didn't know if his organization was facing those challenges; however, if they were, here's how I would address them as their CIO. I closed by saying I would welcome a conversation to learn more about their organization and their industry, whether they had a position for me or not. I included my resume.

A few weeks later, the CEO of one of my former employers called me. He had received a call from a business connection of his: the CEO of the senior living community I had contacted. That CEO wanted to know from my previous CEO if I was "for real" and if he should talk to me. He assured him that I was and that he should. Creativity can work!

Creativity Begets Creativity

Speaking of Top Ten Lists, here are ten examples of creative ways candidates landed an interview. Try one or two that resonate with you. Use the list to think of your own ideas.

Appeal to the Sweet Tooth

Drop off your resume with a box of donuts for the HR department or the hiring manager's department. It is certain to get your resume noticed. Make sure your resume is attached to the box, so they do not become separated before they reach your intended sweet tooth.

Solve a Problem for Them

Put together a slide deck on an issue facing the organization or its industry. In the deck, explain how you would solve the problem. You can kick this one up a notch by putting it online with your talk track included.

Volunteer

This can work especially well if the target company is a nonprofit, but it can also work in commercial enterprises. Give them a try-it-before-you-buy-it offer. Offer to work in the position for thirty days as a volunteer. Hey, the job's open, and you aren't doing anything anyway (other than your full-time job of finding your next job).

Add Some Bling

Upgrade your resume. Add some flair. Upgrade the paper. Add a cover. No, not a cover letter—a really nice cover. Speaking of the paper, use color (make sure it is still easy to read) to help your resume "pop."

Create a Proposal

Similar to the "solve a problem" idea, send a ninety-day plan with your resume. What do you see as the major activities of your first three months in that role? Hit the ground running! Make sure this is targeted to them. Don't send a generic ninety-day plan.

Become a Video Star

Seriously. If a picture is worth 1,000 words, a video is worth 10,000 or more. Create a video. Tell your story. You've worked hard on your story, and it's hard for that to come through on a resume. Post your video on YouTube. Put the link on your resume and in all correspondence with the company. Share the video on your social media channels.

Get Social...Again

Engage with the company on social media. Comment on their content. Share their content. Tag them in relevant content. Recommend others in your social network follow them. If they conduct Twitter chats, join in. You'll be doing two things: research and getting noticed.

Get Social...on Steroids

Take out a Google ad or Facebook ad targeting the company. I urge caution with this one. Google and Facebook ads can be tricky. You want to be sure the company will see it. While you can set spending limits for your ad, you can burn through your budget very quickly with nothing to show for it if the wrong people are clicking on your ad.

Website

Create your own website. Talk about your personal brand, share your accomplishments. Start a blog and write about topics specific to an industry. Become a thought leader. Write a post about the target company based on your research. Write about what they are doing to differentiate in the market. Uploaded your resume so it is downloadable for visitors to your site. Promote your website on social media.

Chocolate

This takes the donut idea a step further. Print your resume on the wrapper of a chocolate bar. Yes, seriously. Be sure to include your contact information and a link to a downloadable version of your resume. Loading a chocolate bar into an applicant tracking system can be a little messy!

And a Bonus: Create a Newsletter

Create a newsletter to update the people in your network on your progress. Who have you talked with this week? Where have you applied? Which companies had you in for an interview? Add some personal news about how you are spending your time. This accomplishes a couple of things. First, it keeps you top of mind with those in your network. Second, it may trigger an introduction, referral, or reference thought in the mind of the recipient.

Go Ahead, Get Your Creative On!

There you have eleven creative ways to get your resume noticed. The internet is filled with other ideas—some good and some creepy…very creepy. Know of other creative ways to get noticed? I'd love to hear from you. Send your creative ways to get your resume noticed to Jeff.Ton@TonEnterprisesLLC.com.

Update Your Resume

Think about the conversations you have been having about your dream job. What words are you using to describe it? What words do the others in your network use?

Think about the research you have been doing on LinkedIn, Twitter, Facebook, and Instagram. What words are being used there to describe the types of roles you are seeking?

Who are the thought leaders in your industry? What are they writing? What words are they using? What problems are they solving?

Who are the future-thinkers in your industry, the ones who write about problems and solutions two and three years down the road? What words are they using?

Pull out your Resume Amplifier. Review the keywords. Are there any that are outdated? Are there new words being used today? Are there new problems being discussed today? The truth is that even though you used current job descriptions in developing your Resume Amplifier, those job descriptions could have been written a year or more before you saw them.

Many times, in large organizations, job descriptions are updated at the beginning of a budget year, when the headcount gets approved. Other times, the hiring manager may just dust off the prior job description, take a quick glance at it, and think, *Yeah, that looks about right*, without taking the time to think about what new needs they have for that role. Thinking, *I can cover that in an interview*.

Update the keywords and skills in your Resume Amplifier. Update your resumes with these skills and keywords.

Don't lay claim to skills you don't have, but be sure you are using current terminology.

Now, pick up your Accomplishment Amplifier. Do any of your accomplishments speak better to those new requirements than the ones you have been using in your Resume Amplifier and, therefore, your resumes? If so, you got it: Update your Resume Amplifier and your resumes!

Finally, in doing this review, are you finding that new skills are required for your dream job, skills that you may not have experience in? Identify a training plan to get those new skills. Sign up for classes, read some books, attend some webinars. Add those education experiences to your resume. Post them proudly to social media.

Reflection

Now's the time for some soul searching. If you've been at your search for weeks that have turned into months, spend some time with your Transition Journal and try to answer the question "Why?" Are you putting in the work? Are you networking? Are you including the two asks? Are you following up with your connections? Should you expand your network? Expand your criteria? Are you getting interviews but not offers? Perhaps you need some interview help.

10

The First Date and Beyond

You've put in the work. You've talked with your confidants. You're filled with excitement. You go to the closet to pick out what to wear. You get dressed. Nervous anticipation replaces the excitement you had a moment ago. As you get in your car, you notice your palms are sweaty. *Yes!* You've gotten the first…interview! What did you think I was talking about?

Time for your first interview for what might be your dream job. As they say, you only get one chance to make a first impression. Let's make sure you are ready.

Preparation Is Key

Gee, where have I heard that before? Well, whoever said that was very wise because it applies here as well.

By now, you have updated your "deal" in your CRM or other tracking tool. You've gathered some research on the company and on the position. It looks promising. Once your first date—uh, interview gets scheduled, you need to tune your research.

Back to Social

Create a stream in your social media aggregator (as a reminder, I use Hootsuite) using keywords to narrow in on the industry or sector the company operates within. Set up another stream for the company itself. You will want to capture both what the company is saying and what others are saying about the company. Finally, set up another stream to capture what the interviewers you will be meeting with are posting.

Spend some time each day reviewing the streams. Read the links. Take notes. Jot down questions. Learn. Study.

Google the industry, the company, and the interviewers. What can you learn through the search results? Repeat this every day. What new information reveals itself? Take notes. Jot down questions.

Research the competition—the company's competition, not your competition. Set up a stream that captures what they are saying (and what others are saying about them). Review that stream every day. Follow the links. Read the content. Take notes. Jot questions.

Visit the competition's website. Compare it to your target company's website. Where are they similar? Where are they differentiated? Guess what? Take notes. Jot questions.

Use LinkedIn to connect with people at similar companies in similar roles. Reach out and ask for a short phone call. Find out what a day in the life is like in that role for that company. Ask if they know the company you are targeting. What can they tell you about your future employer? I hate to repeat. I hate to repeat (see what I did there?), but be sure to take notes and jot down questions that come to mind.

Does all this work work? Absolutely! You will be the most prepared candidate your future company interviews.

My Story

In a previous chapter, I told the story of receiving a job description for an opening from two different people in my network on the same day after having coffee with them the week prior. Let's pick up the story.

The position was for chief information officer at Goodwill Industries of Central Indiana. The job description was amazing. Incredibly detailed. Roles, responsibilities, and requirements to be sure. It also had critical success factors and derailers. It was a gold mine of keywords, skills, and information to build stories around for the interview. I applied. I also sent an email to the head of HR, who was listed on the job description.

I was granted an interview. A first date!

I ate my own dog food and followed the advice I just gave you. As I did my research, I learned the history of the company. I read about the CEO and his background (BTW, he was also the hiring manager, if I got that far). I uncovered a lot of information about the industry, the company's position in the industry, the interviewers…I did it all and had a lot of information.

One of the things I quickly learned was the organization was one of 185 independently owned organizations that shared the same brand. Not a franchise model, but more of a membership model. Organizations around the globe choose to be members and agree to uphold the tenets of the brand. What did this mean? It meant there were 184 other CIOs out there. I furiously started connecting with as many as I could find on LinkedIn.

One of the CIOs who accepted my request was Jim Andreoni. Jim was the CIO for the Goodwill organization in Milwaukee. I asked for thirty minutes of his time, letting him know I was interviewing for the position. He agreed! Though the call was scheduled for thirty minutes, Jim was gracious enough that we talked for almost an hour. One tidbit I learned (in addition to a lot of great information) was that the Milwaukee Goodwill was the largest in the world. The Goodwill of Central Indiana was a distant number two.

Later, at the first interview, I made the statement, "I reached out to Jim Andreoni at the Goodwill in Milwaukee."

They were floored, to say the least. "You spoke with Jim Andreoni?"

"Yes, I wanted to understand a day in the life of a CIO at Goodwill. He and I spoke about some of the challenges he is facing. Now, I don't know if you are facing some of those same challenges, but here's how I would address them."

I'd like to say they hired me on the spot, but that would be a lie. However, after several more rounds of interviews (each round applying the same principles of research), I got the job. It *was* my dream job (and I mean that sincerely).

The Question

You know the one. The question that you fear the most in an interview. You have a gap in your skills you hope they don't ask about. Or, you've had a gap in your employment history. Or maybe you have moved from job to job a lot at points in your career. Maybe you were only with your previous employer for a few months. You *hate* to answer that question. You *hope* it does not come up. When it does, you fumble for an answer. Your uncomfortableness shows like the coffee stain on your shirt you tried to get out before the interview.

Preparation, preparation, preparation. Write down

THE FIRST DATE AND BEYOND

your answer. Memorize it. Rehearse it. Rehearse it until it rolls off your tongue as naturally as your own name.

For me, that question is related to my education. It comes in many forms. "You don't list a degree on your resume. What is your degree?" Or, "Where did you receive your master's?" Or even, "Where did you go to school?" Sometimes I am stunned that thirty or forty years after I would have graduated from college, that question still gets asked, but it does.

My answer?

> Well, it was the seventies. The only thing I ever wanted to be when I grew up was a rock star. No, seriously. I wrote music, played guitar, it's all I ever wanted to do. I even went to Indiana State to major in music theory and composition. I learned something that very first semester. You had to have talent…and I did not. I wasn't sure what I wanted to do. I dropped out, intending to return when I figured it out.
>
> I got married. We had a son (in that order, by the way). I worked while my wife finished her degree, intending to return when she graduated.
>
> And then I discovered computers. The Commodore 64 to be exact. I bought one and fell in love. I devoured everything I could find about computers. I loved to write code. I read college textbooks on database theory and design; system development life cycle, PL/I, COBOL, IMS…everything. Honestly, by the time I could return to school, I was

> teaching community college courses in computer science and programming. I convinced myself I didn't need to go back.
>
> In fact, I never went back. But, let me tell you how I turned that experience in a passion for lifelong learning…

Humor, a bit tongue-in-cheek, a bit self-deprecating… but sincere, honest, and relatable. I turned the question I dreaded into a positive answer about lifelong learning and what that would mean for them should they hire me.

I am not advocating that others follow that educational path. It has been a difficult journey. I do regret not having a degree. It has created many roadblocks in my career. Yes, I was able to overcome them and rise to the level of a CIO and later an executive at a tech company, but I would not do it again.

Faux Pas

While we are on the topic of interviewing, let's talk about recovering from a faux pas, a false step. You can recover from missteps (well, some missteps) in the interview process. As in "*the* question," it's how you talk about the error or omission or oversight. You address it head-on. With sincerity. And you use it to show your personal brand and how you will handle errors as an employee.

Recoverable missteps can be as benign as misstating a fact in the interview, calling the interviewer by the wrong name, or getting lost in responding to a question. The key to recovery in these situations is to correct it as soon as you realize it. That may be immediately, later in the interview, or even after the interview is over.

There are other mistakes that are harder to overcome,

but not impossible. You might be a bit rusty if you have not interviewed in some time. It is a good idea to rehearse, but even then, you may be nervous or uncomfortable. It's okay. Fess up. Admit this is your first interview in several years. If it is not, and you still come across as nervous, fess up to that as well. "I find one of the most difficult things to do is to sell myself, so please bear with me. However, I am quite capable of selling my ideas or the ideas of my team…"

Some errors are so egregious they are almost impossible to overcome. These come in a variety of forms, such as bad-mouthing previous employers, defensive responses to questions, dishonesty, and focusing on what you want from them rather than what you can do for them. Should you have an off day and realize you really blew the interview by committing one of these offenses or something similar, reflect on it. Write in your journal, answering the question "Why?" I also recommend writing a thank-you note and owning up to the error. Apologize and move on.

My Own Faux Pas

I once missed an entire interview and was able to not only recover but get the job!

I had applied for an executive role by emailing the VP of HR directly. His response was swift. "Let's talk Monday at 9 AM, I will call you at the number on your resume." *Wow!* I could not be more excited.

The role *was* my dream job! The company checked every box on my Next Company Top Ten List. The job description was practically an overlay of my resume and checked every box on my Next Position Top Ten List. AND, the guy responded right away!

Monday came. I sat down in my home office. Plugged

in my BlackBerry (yeah, I know) and waited. No call at 9 a.m. No call at 9:05. I checked my email. Yes, it said he was to call me. Okay, perhaps a meeting ran long, no worries, just be patient. No call at 9:10. By now I was so nervous I was about to jump out of my skin. No call at 9:15…9:20…I checked my email again.

There at the top of my inbox was an email from my son. "Dad, is something wrong? I've been texting you all morning and you aren't responding."

What? I haven't received any texts! I checked my phone…no texts…ringer on…uh, wait. *No service? What?!?!* Yep, my phone was not connected to the cellular network. *Crap!* (To be honest, I used a stronger word.) I rebooted my phone. It immediately reconnected to the network. *Bing, bing, bing.* My son's text messages came in. *Bing, bing*…uh, *that* is a voice mail. Petrified, I checked my voice mail. Sure enough, not one, not two, but *three* messages. "Hello, Jeff. This is Joe Smith calling from Roadrunner for our 9 a.m. call. I will try back."

I frantically called his office. Now I got voice mail. *Crap!* (Insert your favorite expletive; I probably used them all.) I left a message apologizing profusely, explained what happened, and asked if we could set up a new time.

Nothing. No return call.

I sent him an email.

Nothing. No return email.

To say I was devastated was an understatement. Days went by. A week. Two.

I was driving one afternoon, and my cell phone rang. It was a recruiter. He was working on the position for Roadrunner. He wanted to schedule a time for me to interview with him. Two emotions at once. Ecstatic I was back in the game. Disappointed I had been relegated to the B-team. No offense to my recruiter friends, but I had a direct line with the VP of HR, and now I am in the stack with everyone else. Ugh!

I passed the interview and was given a face-to-face with…the VP of HR. I had my apology speech already. I walked into his office; we shake hands and sit down. He looks at me with a cold stare and says, "I'd like to start by talking about telecommunications."

"Well," I said, "as a candidate you are always looking for a way to stand out from the other candidates, but missing an interview due to a technology issue probably isn't the best way to make an impression for a CIO."

He started laughing. I started laughing (nervously). I then apologized again.

I got the job!

After the Interview

When you get home after the interview, take a moment to review your notes (you did take notes, didn't you?). Expand your notes, if need be. I know I, for one, jot brief one- or two-word notes. If I don't go back and review and expand on my thoughts soon after taking notes, later I won't even be able to read them, much less remember what they meant.

After completing your notes, take the time to write thank-you notes to each person who interviewed you. Email is fine enough, but a handwritten note will leave a great impression with the interviewer. In the thank-you note, reference your notes and write something specific. You could expand on an answer you had given them, mention one or two things you discussed with them, or provide them with the title of a book or article that would be meaningful based on your conversation.

The note will carry a bigger impact if you can recall a personal detail that had come up in the interview. Perhaps, as an icebreaker, you had mentioned the university plaque hanging on their wall, or the picture of their dog, or a book on their shelf. Refer to that in your note. A word of caution: If you didn't talk about the picture of their kids on their desk, don't bring them up now…that's creepy.

Of course, after you have written all your thank-you notes, update your CRM with the new status. As you're updating your CRM, add a note that scores the company, the position, and the hiring manager (if you met them in the process) against your Top Ten Lists. Which items do they check off? Where are the gaps? The gaps can serve as questions to dig into during your next interview.

Reflection

Interviews are a great prompt for writing in your journal. Journaling should be different from expanding on your notes. In your journal, write your thoughts and feelings. Focus on the time in the interview itself. How did you do? Where could you improve? Now, a few hours later, how do you feel about the interview?

11

The End Game

What's the end game? To land your dream job, of course! You've put in the work. You've landed interviews. You've aced interviews. Finally, it pays off. You get the phone call you've been waiting for since you started this process way back in chapter 1. "Jill, we would love for you to join us at Roadrunner. We will be mailing you a written offer today, but let me give you the high points."

Success! You've Gotten the Offer

It is time to celebrate. Almost. Okay, maybe it does warrant a fist pump or two, or at least a smile. The truth is, evaluating an offer can be complex. But you are ready. You've done the work. You should take a brief pause at this point. All the networking you have done was to get you an interview. All the interviewing you did was to get you an offer. You've taken the next step on your journey to find your dream job.

First, let's revisit your Top Ten Lists on your SOM Amplifier. How many boxes does the position check? How about the company? The hiring manager? Which boxes are checked can be more important than how many. For example, in reviewing your Next Company Top Ten List, you find the organization checks six of ten. That's pretty good, right? What if they are the bottom six on your list? They are missing the top four priorities you want in your dream job.

If you are using the downloaded version of the SOM Amplifier, make a copy of the form. Next to each of your Top Ten List items, check each one met by this company. Tally the points for each checked row. That sum is the weighted score. If the company achieves all ten items, their score would be 55. In the example above, they would receive a 21. Not even half.

What about the other Top Ten Lists? Continue checking the boxes for the Next Position and Next Boss Top Ten Lists. How did they fare there?

With one offer on the table, you will have to make the call. I can't make that decision for you. (Sorry!) Do you wait to see if you get another offer? Do you accept this one knowing you are making some tradeoffs against your dream job? A lot will depend on how long your search has lasted thus far, how active your interviewing has been, and how long you can wait.

What if they've gotten a high score on your Top Ten List, say a 45 or higher on each list, or you've decided to continue despite a low score on one of the lists? There are several more things to evaluate in your offer. Some of them may or may not have been on your Top Ten Lists. Remember, you only have one offer at this point, so you have nothing to compare against.

- **Salary:** How does the salary compare in the market? Is it what you expected?
- **Other compensation:** Is there a bonus? Is it acceptable? How is it determined? Is it based on your performance or the performance of the company?
- **Benefits:** Healthcare coverage and costs can vary widely. Be sure you understand the options. Is there a 401(k)? What is the matching? Are there other profit-sharing opportunities?
- **Other benefits:** Vacation, flexible work schedule, work from home policy, other benefits?

Of course, at this point, many of these things are up for negotiation. You won't be able to negotiate every item in the offer. Identify the elements that are most important to you.

Negotiations can be nerve-racking, especially if you are not accustomed to the dance of negotiation. The Resources section at the back of the book lists some resources to help you master the art of negotiation.

Lucky You! You Have Multiple Offers!

Congratulations! As I always say, "A choice of one isn't really a choice at all." But now you have choices. Multiple offers have come in. Congratulations on each one!

Your first step is to evaluate each offer independently. Use the process described above.

Now, it's time to compare the offers. How did they score on your Top Ten Lists? Was one a clear winner in points? How many number ones did it check off? Is there a clear winner in your gut?

Compare the other components of the offer (salary, bonus, etc.). Does one stand out over the others?

Divide the offers into three categories:

- **Negotiate.** These are the offers you definitely want to take to the next step;
- **Reject.** These offers are so far off the mark there is no way, even through negotiation, to make them viable; and,
- **Hold.** These offers you will do your best to keep "warm" while you negotiate with those in the first category.

Once you have decided to reject an offer, contact the company and politely turn down the offer. Provide them with feedback on where the offer missed the mark (or marks). Be ready for them to try to turn it into a negotiation. Stand firm on your decision.

For the offers in the Hold category, as your response timeline nears an end, reach out and tell them you are evaluating multiple offers and you'd like a bit more time. Many times, if you ask for a reasonable extension, they will accommodate it. In my experience, you can only extend once. If they will not give you more time, you will have to respectfully decline the offer.

By now, you should have one or two or no more than three offers you would like to negotiate. Once again, identify the elements that are most important to you; these may be different in the different offers.

As you negotiate, you can use one offer to negotiate the other. For example, "Susan, I really want to work for Roadrunner. I believe I can add significant value to the organization. I must be honest, however; I have another offer that comes with a salary and compensation package that is 5 percent higher than the offer from Roadrunner. Would you entertain matching that comp package?"

This is a fair tactic in negotiation. What is not fair is saying you have another offer when, in fact, you don't. *That* does not exhibit high integrity and can come back to bite you. I also advise against revealing who made the other offer. If asked, you could say, "I'd prefer not to mention who the company is. My offer from them, like the offer from you, is confidential."

You Got the Job! Your Dream Job!

Now is the time to celebrate. Congratulations. You have worked hard, and you deserve it!

After you are done celebrating…that's okay…I'll wait.

After you are done celebrating, there are still some things for you to do.

Send a note to the hiring manager. Thank them for putting their trust in you. Tell them how excited you are to join them. Ask if there is anything you can do for them between now and day one on the job. It's a nice touch.

Contact the other companies you were in negotiation with to tell them you have accepted an offer. Thank them very much for the time they invested in you and the process.

Next, contact all the companies where you are actively interviewing. Thank them for their time.

You're not done thanking people yet!

Send an update to everyone you networked with during this time. Tell them about your new role. Thank them for their help and support. Ask if there is anything you can do for them. If you have been sending a newsletter update to your network, you can use that to let people know and to thank them.

Finally, I want you to pledge two things. First, never let your network go cold. You've worked hard to build an amazing network of friends, colleagues, peers, and industry gurus. Keep it going! It will continue to pay dividends for the rest of your career.

Second, whenever anyone asks you to network and help them in their career, your answer should be "Yes, what time and where?" Well, maybe you tell them when you are available, but you get the idea. Set aside time to meet with people in transition. Give them advice.

Oh, and one other thing. I would love to hear about your new dream job. Send me a note at Jeff.Ton@TonEnterprisesLLC.com. I want to hear your story!

Reflection

This chapter, this book, would not be complete without some reflection. Write in your Transition Journal. What are your thoughts about the journey you have just completed? What were the ups? What were the downs? What did you learn? What would you do differently?

You have seen the value in journaling. Keep it up! Start a new journal. Spend some time each day reflecting and writing. Reread your previous entries from time to time. You will be amazed at the new lessons that reveal themselves to you. As you change, the lessons change. It's part of the magic of journaling!

Take care, stay safe, be well,
Jeff

Bibliography

Arbinger Institute. *Leadership and Self-Deception: Getting out of the Box*. Berrett-Koehler Publishers, 2018.

Barnaby, Jason. *Igniting the Fire Starter Within: The Secrets to Finding Your Fire, Fanning Your Flame, and Tending Your Tribe*. CreateSpace, 2019.

Berninger, Virginia W., et al. "Early Development of Language by Hand: Composing, Reading, Listening, and Speaking Connections; Three Letter-Writing Modes; and Fast Mapping in Spelling." *Developmental Neuropsychology* 29, no. 1 (2006): 61–92. doi:10.1207/s15326942dn2901_5.

Biehl, Bobb. *Maximising Your Strengths, Making Your Weaknesses Irrelevant*. BobbBiehl.com.

Drucker, Peter F. *Classic Drucker: Essential Wisdom of Peter Drucker from the Pages of Harvard Business Review*. Harvard Business Press, 2006. P. 3.

Nguyen, Thai. "10 Surprising Benefits of Keeping a Journal." HuffPost, December 7, 2017. www.huffpost.com/entry/benefits-of-journaling-_b_6648884.

Schepp, Brad, and Debra Schepp. *How to Find a Job on LinkedIn, Facebook, Twitter, and Google+*. McGraw-Hill, 2012.

Waninger, Amy C. *Network beyond Bias: Making Diversity a Competitive Advantage for Your Career*. Lead at Any Level LLC, 2018.

"What Is Personal Branding [Free Personal Brand Health Checker]." Influencer Marketing Hub, May 16, 2019. influencermarketinghub.com/what-is-personal-branding.

Wood, Orrin G. *The Executive Job Search: A Comprehensive Handbook for Seasoned Professionals*. McGraw-Hill, 2003.

Yate, Martin. "How to Supercharge Your Resume." CareerCast.com, March 9, 2017. www.careercast.com/career-news/how-supercharge-your-resume.

Resources

Resources used throughout this book are available for free download at www.JeffreySTon.com/AYJS/Resources.

Assessments Mentioned

In chapter 2, you are encouraged to take a series of assessments. The ones I recommend are:

- **Strengths:** StrengthsFinder 2.0 (now CliftonStrengths) from Gallup
  https://www.gallup.com/cliftonstrengths/en/strengthsfinder.aspx
- **Values:** Personal Values Assessment from Barrett Values Centre
  https://www.valuescentre.com/tools-assessments/pva
- **Passions:** The Passion Test from GeniusU
  https://thepassiontest.geniusu.com
- **Purpose:** The Sparktype Assessment from the Good Life Project
  https://www.goodlifeproject.com/sparketypes

Purpose HQ

In chapter 2, I mentioned an offer that would help you manage the various assessments you have taken and will take as a part of this journey.

Purpose HQ is an app that enables you to store the results of the assessments mentioned above in one central location. The Purpose HQ also provides access to the following assessments:

- **PAIRIN Mindset:** PAIRIN's soft skills assessment was built upon sixty years of research and seventeen years of job performance measurement by the founders and was co-designed with partners from public education, industry, foundations, and government. The PAIRIN Survey measures over one hundred soft skills and mindsets in seven minutes.
- **Kolbe (fee applies):** Kolbe measures your instinctive way of doing things and the result is called your MO (method of operation). It is the only validated assessment that measures a person's conative strengths. Gain greater understanding of your own human nature and begin the process of maximizing your potential.
- **DiSC (fee applies):** DiSC is a behavior assessment tool based on the DISC theory of psychologist William Moulton Marston, which centers on four different personality traits which are currently Dominance (D), Influence (I), Steadiness (S), and Conscientiousness (C).
- **Predictive Index:** The Predictive Index, also known as the PI Behavioral Assessment, is a pop-

ular pre-employment personality test. Comprised by the Predictive Index company, the test aims to measure a candidate's suitability to a specific position or employer.
- **16 Personalities:** Our personality types are based on five independent spectrums, with all letters in the type code (e.g., INFJ-A) referring to one of the two sides of the corresponding spectrum. You can see where you fall on each scale by completing our free personality assessment, NERIS Type Explorer. This approach has allowed us to achieve high test accuracy while also retaining the ability to define and describe distinct personality types.
- **Enneagram:** The Enneagram is a personality typing system that consists of nine different types. Everyone is considered to be one single type, although one can have traits belonging to other ones. While it's uncertain whether this type is genetically determined, many believe it is already in place at birth.

To take advantage of this offer send me an email at Jeff.Ton@TonEnterprisesLLC.com and ask for Purpose HQ access!

Additional Resources

Here are some books I have found valuable in my own education into the art and skill of negotiation.

- Fisher, Robert, et al. *Getting to Yes: Negotiating Agreement without Giving In*. Penguin Books, 1986.

- *Harvard Business Essentials: Negotiation.* Harvard Business School Press, 2003.
- Voss, Christopher, and Tahl Raz. *Never Split the Difference: Negotiating as If Your Life Depended on It.* Harper Business, 2016.

As valuable as those books were, I highly recommend Jared Curhan's "Negotiation Training for Executives" course from MIT Sloan's Executive Education Program (http://executive.mit.edu/openenrollment/program/negotiation-for-executives).

About the Author

Jeff Ton is a sought-after leadership speaker, author, and explorer, having led powerful teams and built successful IT departments for over thirty years. He is the author of *Amplify Your Value* (2018) and hosts the podcast *Status Go*. As a frequent keynote speaker, he has explored topics related to the evolving IT landscape and the changing role of the CIO.

Jeff served in various roles with Thomson Multimedia (RCA) for over fourteen years. He then guided technology and business strategy as chief information officer for Lauth Property Group and later for Goodwill Industries of Central & Southern Indiana. Until early in 2020, Jeff was senior vice president of product and strategic alliances at InterVision. There he thrived on developing people while driving the company's product strategy, service vision, and strategic approach.

Throughout his career, Jeff has mentored, coached, and guided hundreds of professionals in their careers. His strategies of first looking to self, building a strong professional network, defining what makes a dream job, and then locating that dream job have enabled countless professionals to find their dream jobs.

Meet Jeff and learn more at www.JeffreySTon.com.

Join my weekly newsletter for thought-provoking insights delivered straight to your inbox every Tuesday! You'll receive:

- **Timely Musings**: Insights and lessons learned throughout the week
- **Readers' Q&A**: My response to someone's recent question
- **Success Spotlight**: Highlight of a person or company helping others grow
- **Rivers of Thought**: A more personal observation or musing on a topic

Subscribe Now
https://mailchi.mp/jeffreyston.com/leadershipinsights

Also by Jeffrey S. Ton

*Amplify Your Value:
Leading IT with Strategic Vision*

Are you an IT leader who struggles to make your voice heard? Does your company's executive team leave you out of important meetings? Are your business ideas and opinions never taken seriously? Keynote speaker and IT visionary Jeff Ton has thirty-five years of experience helping companies build strategic technology plans and innovative practices. His transformative methods will guide you and your department in transitioning from "the computer guys" to the heart of the business.

Amplify Your Value is a must-have reference for IT heads who are ready to take their leadership skills to the next level. If you like systematic action plans, innovative management, and real-world examples, then you'll love Jeff Ton's insightful guide.

Buy now at
https://jeffreyston.com/author-amplify-your-value

"Jeff tells a compelling story of being a CIO in the trenches—taking charge when opportunities present themselves, shoring up operations when required, and evolving strategies that drive business results. IT leaders will relate to his challenges and learn best practices from an experienced leader."

—**Isaac Sacolick**
President and CIO of StarCIO and
author of *Driving Digital*

www.ingramcontent.com/pod-product-compliance
Lightning Source LLC
Chambersburg PA
CBHW021103080526
44587CB00010B/354